AN ACTOR SUCCEEDS

Other books by Boze Hadleigh

Broadway Babylon
Celluloid Gaze
Hollywood Gays
Celebrity Feuds!
Mexico's Most Wanted
Celebrity Diss and Tell

AN ACTOR SUCCEEDS

Tips, Secrets, and Advice
on Auditioning, Connecting,
Coping, and Thriving
in and out of Hollywood,
from Stars, Agents, Coaches,
Casting People, Directors,
Producers, and Others

Boze Hadleigh

APPLAUSE
THEATRE & CINEMA BOOKS

AN IMPRINT OF HAL LEONARD CORPORATION

Published in 2014 by Applause Theatre & Cinema Books
An Imprint of Hal Leonard Corporation
7777 West Bluemound Road
Milwaukee, WI 53213

Trade Book Division Editorial Offices
33 Plymouth St., Montclair, NJ 07042

Printed in the United States of America

Book design by Michael Kellner

Library of Congress Cataloging-in-Publication Data is available upon request.

ISBN 978-0-87910-888-5

www.applausebooks.com

TO RONNIE

"I tell the newer actors to be starstruck in the smart way: if stardom comes your way, it's a bonus; but if not, you still have the pleasure of doing what you love."
—MERYL STREEP

_____

"Fame is a double-edged sword. But real success is a lifelong satisfaction nobody can take away from you."
—MARLON BRANDO

_____

"The world is a stage, yes. The trick, though, is to get paid and praised for the acting you do." —ARTHUR MILLER

Contents

Acknowledgments

M ost special thanks to Ronald Boze Stockwell and Linda Fresia. And to John Cerullo, Bernadette Malavarca, Jaime Nelson, Wes Seeley, Mary Vandenberg, and the whole Applause team. Also Harry Benshoff, E. J. Fleming, Cris Franco, Lorri Jean, Max Ksenjak, Darrin Nogales, Chad Oberhausen, Shaun Pelofsky, Dale Reynolds, Anne Salvatore, Peter Shelley, Howard Smith and David Wright, Mary Stark, Don Weise, and Wendy Westgate.

Introduction

Aristotle said theater is medicine. He meant acting, for back then, theater was all of acting—professional acting, as opposed to the acting we each do most every day of our lives. Acting can be a tonic for those who go to see it or press a button to see it. Like books (though seldom as in-depth), movies, programs, and plays can transport us to other places, yield new experiences and insights, raise questions, stir emotions, and move our hearts.

Acting is also medicine for the actor. Everyone's heard about actors sustaining high fevers or injuries who went on with the show, gave the audience their money's worth, and only felt pain *after* the performance. Proving how much of suffering, and transcending it, is in the mind. Acting, too, is in the mind—an imaginative, focused mind that delves into a given character's identity and circumstances.

More than a few actors enter the field to become other people. Whether to expand themselves, provide emotional outlets, or try and escape themselves, playing someone else may be therapeutic, uninhibiting, exploratory, or just plain fun. Plus you get paid for it! Of course, some acting involves more of a stretch, and some actors stretch more than others. But few actors today, including above-the-title ones, are content to dwell in the cult of personality, as did so many golden-age movie stars.

Playing heroes, antiheroes, and villains, people like and unlike oneself, is a welcome challenge for most performers. But getting hired to do so is the quandary in today's so-competitive, overcrowded market. The lure of fame and fortune draws an increasing percentage of the population, often with no qualification besides looks or drive, to Hollywood and sometimes New York, since theater is no longer the unquestioned training ground for tomorrow's names.

Make no mistake: looks are often still a qualification. At first. Once the first bloom of youth fades, personality and talent are required. The latter becomes crucial if one wants to stay in the game. A heartening fact for the committed actor is that within five years, most newbies—on either coast and in between—drop out. The biz is just too difficult for them, or things didn't happen quickly enough.

Acting classes and film schools usually teach the basics but tend to leave out most of the practical, elusive advice and tips that can make a new actor's post-class, beyond-school life much easier. For an acting career entails not just your character interacting with other characters, it's you, the job-hungry actor (or the actor wanting to be hired more often), learning to deal with the myriad necessary people—most of them not actors!—in "the industry."

The following one thousand or so secrets, tips, and pieces of advice—culled from hundreds of books, memoirs, and articles (mostly but not all in English); from television, the Internet, and radio; and from classes, lectures, personal interviews, correspondence, and clippings galore—should provide new and not-so-new actors with useful information that (particularly for younger actors) might otherwise take years to find out, sometimes the hard way.

May the enclosed deliver an occasional grin or chuckle—after all, acting professionally is tougher than it looks, and getting work is even harder. More crucially, may it help you to audition, connect, work, and cope more successfully. To paraphrase Stanislavski's classic text *An Actor Prepares*, may this book help the actor reading it prepare for success. . . .

SEPTEMBER 12, 2013
BEVERLY HILLS, CALIFORNIA

1

ACTING

"I hate to say this, but if you can convincingly tell a lie, you can act." —SANFORD MEISNER, acting coach

"I was kind of shocked when someone told me the ancient Greeks had the same word for 'liar' as for 'actor.' Then I thought about it . . . it makes sense!"
—LUCY LIU

"Long ago I told a harmless lie—you know, to spare someone's feelings. And you know how some people say you can always tell if a person's lying, 'cause he won't look you in the eye? Untrue! That's when I started realizing I had the makings of a thespian."
—JOHNNY DEPP

"There's that lyric [Stephen] Sondheim wrote about an actress who felt she should have gone to an acting school, but somebody said, 'She's sincere.' There's a lot to that . . . I think it was George Burns who said if you can fake sincerity, you can make it in show business." —CAROL BURNETT

"I was thrust into my profession without any training whatsoever. . . . So one day I said to Jimmy Cagney, 'Jimmy, what is acting?' and he said, 'I don't know. All I can tell you is, whatever you say, mean it,' and I thought that was marvelous counsel." —OLIVIA DE HAVILLAND, two-time Oscar winner

"If you can prevaricate while looking somebody in the eye, you can move on to become an actor. Acting requires believability, which many people have, but also engaging them—not avoiding looking them in the eye. Whether flirting or lying or confessing, an actor must fully engage with the other character and, thereby, with each individual audience member." —Sir MICHAEL REDGRAVE

"Sir Laurence Olivier was directing Marilyn Monroe in *The Prince and the Showgirl*. He thought her performance was nothing, that she was hardly acting, unlike him, with his big voice and gestures. But when he saw the rushes, he realized she would steal the film. Her face and what it quietly yet powerfully expressed made her performance more vivid and interesting. He was the better stage actor, but she was the better movie actor." —CLAUDE CHAGRIN, French mime

"Two prototypes, when it comes to female movie stars: a Liz Taylor, who's usually not smiling, and a Marilyn Monroe, who usually is. The former lasts longer, but the latter is better loved and remembered." —JOHN SPRINGER, publicist

"Some performers are smarter than they seem, in particular the smart cookies who play dumb blondes. I had the pleasure of working more than once with the charming and highly intelligent Judy Holliday. One time, her mother was visiting the set, and Judy admitted that she hadn't begun speaking until a very late age. 'How old was I when I started talking, Mom?'

"Her mother answered, 'Three or four.'

"'What were my first words?'

"'Please adjust the venetian blind.'" —JACK LEMMON

"When you go to a play in its third month or so, you're impressed by the freshness of a good actor, who sounds the same as on the first or second night or the third week. In a movie, for all you know, that great scene required 20 or more takes. The point and the great satisfaction is mastering that skill, learning to create that illusion of freshness." —DAVID MCCALLUM (*NCIS*)

"Being able to repeat something good is real power—the power an actor strives for. On the stage, where repetition is each night's duty, an emotion and its sincerity must be strong enough to be re-created. Once-in-a-blue-moon inspiration is wonderful, but fleeting. Permanent craft and its ability to present special moments afresh is invaluable." —KATHARINE CORNELL, dubbed the "First Lady of the American Stage" by critic Alexander Woollcott

"I was looking at real, live people on a stage. But even in the back row, it was from the mesmerizing distance of their creative, convincing imagination and my willing, hopeful belief. At times it was like hypnosis. Or magic! It was so much more vivid and thrilling than the dull everyday world. So an actress I absolutely had to become!" —CAROL CHANNING

"I finally wrote a book. In part, it tells how my childhood and youth were often, shall we say, terrible. Nothing like what people assume about the smiling blonde actress who played mom to 'The Brady Bunch.' It was performing that saved my life, that gave me a reason to sometimes want to continue my life at all." —FLORENCE HENDERSON

"My mom and I would go to the movies when I was little. When we came home, one of the main characters would have made an impression on me—I didn't choose which character—and I'd start acting like a cross between myself and him, occasionally her. For a while after each movie, part of me was inhabited

by what I'd seen and experienced on the screen."
—JOHN TRAVOLTA

"When my mother got home from work she would take me to the movies . . . I'd go home and act out all the parts. It had a tremendous influence on my becoming an actor." —AL PACINO

"When you're very convincing as a particular character, a lot of people assume that's the real you. I can't do much about that. But I do avoid taking a character home with me. Some actors become their character for the duration of shooting. Not me. I'm me, except on set or on location. It's too complicated otherwise, and not fair to the 'civilians' around me!" —JESSICA CHASTAIN (*Zero Dark Thirty*)

"It was undeniably a form of escape, yet also a kind of creativity. When I was at the movies, I never identified with the star. It was with the character—the character and her life and problems, her drama and relationships. I wanted to explore that." —BARBRA STREISAND

"What impressed me was the sheer force of some personalities. [Barbara] Stanwyck was one—the star of my first movie. She was tough, dominant, forceful. Some people are background people—in real life—and some are front-and-center. . . . It's surprising how many people take a backseat in the vehicle that is their

own life. I decided that if I was going to act, I'd have to be a star actor. Nothing wrong with not being a star, but for me it would have been embarrassing."
—KIRK DOUGLAS

"Sure, I got my foot in the door thanks to my looks. But I think I'm a better actor than I'm given credit for. They say the camera never lies. It does. . . ."
—ROCK HUDSON, who played only heterosexuals in some 60 movies

"Your usual personality in your daily life is not necessarily what you play or become known for. In the old days you had actors who played nothing but villains, yet in real life they could be sweethearts or milquetoasts. A lot of it has to do with what you're assigned." —KEVIN SPACEY (*The Usual Suspects*)

"If we're honest, we each have several sides or facets. Mostly hidden, and mostly out of the paltry fear of the judgment of strangers. . . . You think it wasn't fun being Liberace [in *Behind the Candelabra*]? I'm sure he had a ball being Liberace! As an actor, I can have fun and actually get paid to act in an uninhibited way that I'd never dare in real life, especially not outside the home." —MICHAEL DOUGLAS

"I had always felt a freedom and a sense of assuredness when I was on stage that I never felt as a human being." —KARL MALDEN (*Dead Ringer*)

"Put me in a supermarket and I can get intimidated by a pushy clerk or cashier. Put me in front of a camera and give me Tony Soprano's dialogue, and I'm off to the races!" —JAMES GANDOLFINI

"Everyone in New York and Hollywood talks about talent. There's far less talk about the luck needed for that breakthrough role that makes you famous and your talent apparent. That's up to casting, directing, producing and, yes, writing people, plus your being in the right place at the right time. Luck is an essential." —PETER FONDA (*Easy Rider*)

"An individual, an actor, has a certain amount of talent. Of course, the more, the better. But it still needs to be developed into a craft, so that if opportunity comes knocking, you can shine instead of falter. Unfortunately, opportunity doesn't always come knocking. Despite anyone's great talent or looks, nobody is guaranteed a big break, let alone stardom." —VIVIAN VANCE (*I Love Lucy*)

"You better love acting, because you'll be a success if you can make a living at it. Most actors do not. As for becoming a star, that's on a par with winning the lottery it's possible, but it's nearly impossible. Enjoy the level you achieve. The alternative is to become miserable, frustrated, and bitter." —GARRETT MORRIS (*Saturday Night Live*)

"My father loved acting. But he didn't become a big-name, successful actor. When I'm acting, sooner or later I become aware that I'm extending and even completing my father's dream. I think that helps strengthen my acting." —JULIA ROBERTS

"My mother was beautiful . . . an Italian Garbo. Romilda wanted so much to be an actress. She let her parents prevent her. . . . Without my mother, I would not have become a star. Her dream was mine. So I feel like three people: Sofia the grown-up girl, Sophia the movie star, and Romilda the movie star." —SOPHIA LOREN

"My mother's dreams were crushed by the era and the patriarchal society she lived in. I witnessed the end result. I vowed it would never happen to me. Acting became my way of flying above all the limitations that kept most women chained to a small plot of ground." —SHIRLEY MACLAINE

"Growing up, I was ignored. I was a child unheard and little seen. I escaped it, but with a huge need still to go in front of people and know that I will be seen, I will be heard, and I will not stop until I have finished speaking." —SIR BEN KINGSLEY

"I love acting because when it's time to speak everyone else has to shut up before your cue." —FRED WILLARD *(Best in Show)*

"I was quite a forceful child, had to get my own way. So I'd alter my behavior to get it. Sometimes I was passive, sometimes aggressive, sometimes winsome, you name it. I ran the gamut. Those were my first acting lessons—and for free!" —COLLEEN DEWHURST, Actors' Equity president

"Many actors feel circumscribed by roles in which they don't get to exhibit all the emotions they know they're capable of. Some roles, particularly men's roles and more particularly Englishmen's roles, don't boast a wide emotional range. But then, acting isn't always about *acting*." —Dame JUDI DENCH

"Privately, anyone can emote beautifully in front of a mirror. It's having to do it in front of other people that's the real test. To me, that's the primary value of an acting class. It's frankly not so much about taking instruction from people who didn't attain a lot of acting success as about dredging up the necessary emotions in front of an audience and discovering what you are and aren't capable of." —HUGH GRANT

"Many people secretly admire actors yet are relieved they're not [actors themselves], because of how actors sometimes expose themselves . . . having to be emotionally raw or ugly, not to mention physically naked. But most of that doesn't apply to supporting actors or actresses. Nor leading men. Mostly, all of that gets shoved onto leading ladies." —KATE WINSLET, Oscar winner

"I used to worry about having to cry on screen when I got into movies. Could I do it? I needn't have worried —I've never been called on, as an *actor*, to display tears." —ROBERT MITCHUM

"It's not surprising that women tend to be better actors than men. After all, acting is 90 percent reaction, and females spend most of their lives reacting to males." —SUSAN STRASBERG, who played Anne Frank on Broadway

"More and more in films today, it's actors equal just action, and actresses equal just reaction." —JENNIFER ANISTON

"I think the more sensitive you are as a person, the better an actor you can be . . . if you let it out. Not being the eldest kid in my family, and with an alcoholic mother and a brutal father, I had to be aware of other people; I was initially extremely sensitive. Until I learned to hide it . . . and then eventually let it out under the guise of a character I was enacting." —MARLON BRANDO

"You have to hand it to the character actors, then and now. They do more and better acting than most leading men. Only, since they're not on screen as much, you don't always notice." —STEVE BUSCEMI (*Reservoir Dogs*)

"If you aren't thinking and concerned about what to do with your hands on stage, you won't be bothered with them . . . you won't look fake. Forget about your hands; they do their own thing, and much more naturally than if you try and instruct them." —JEFF COREY, actor-coach

"I found that one luxury which camera acting affords is that there's far less need to be concerned with bits of business involving one's hands." —Dame JUDITH ANDERSON (*Rebecca*)

"Too many people worry about close-ups. Don't bother. If you're a character actor, you won't have any. Until and unless you turn out to be the story's murderer and the camera comes in tight for your reaction, if any." —DON SIMPSON, producer (*Beverly Hills Cop*)

"Of course we all learn that acting is basically reacting. The least acting you ever have to do is in a close-up. The close-up may require an actor's reaction, but a small, subtle one. Generally speaking, the less you 'act' in a close-up, the better." —Sir JOHN GIELGUD

"By and large, the close-up is meant to showcase the physical beauty—or in the golden era, perfection—of the lead actress and actor. Second to that, it's there for love scenes—his close-up, her close-up, etc., indicating romantic rapture and then, possibly, sexual ecstasy.

"The third use of a close-up is to move the plot along via mutual reactions." —STIRLING SILLIPHANT, screenwriter (*The Towering Inferno*)

"I found that having a good poker face turned out to be good in close-up shots. And who knew then that someday they'd do whole TV shows of celebrities playing poker? You never know what'll come in handy for your career." —GINA GERSHON (*Bound*)

"I was not delighted that I had such prominent eyes . . . not until I went on the stage, where it became an asset and drew more attention to my character. . . . For the camera, my eyes were again larger than life, so I compensated, as various actresses did, by using lipstick to create bigger lips to balance my features." —BETTE DAVIS

"One thing my acting teachers emphasized was to not roll your eyes—you know, look up toward the ceiling in amazement or disgust. It's a common reaction in everyday life. However it does look exaggerated on actors who're past puberty." —NEIL PATRICK HARRIS (*How I Met Your Mother*)

"Beware overactive eyebrows! Interiorly, you may think they enhance or express emotion. But spectators may think you look comical . . . I'll always remember a successful actor friend who was mentoring me. Rather than ridiculing my eyebrows, as some folks had done, he had me watch one of those Sheikh movies starring Rudolph Valentino. The great sex symbol of the 1920s was supposed to be this forceful and irresistible figure in the desert, yet his bouncing eyebrows made him seem merely comical and a big ham.

"By coincidence, weeks later I saw a lot of *Lawrence of Arabia*—a very long movie!—and not once did I see Peter O'Toole overuse or even hardly use his eyebrows. Those two films were a great lesson, especially the first one."
—ELLE MACPHERSON, who played models in four of her first seven movies

"As an acting coach, it's often easier to impress upon a student what not to do than what to do. That is due to fear, which is probably an actor's greatest motivator." —UTA HAGEN, acting coach

"Love performing, hate failure, ignore rejection."
—JENNIFER LOPEZ's cardinal rules for success

"An aspiring actor cannot afford to be obnoxious—unless he or she is beautiful and has relatives in the business. Even then. . . . But what an aspiring actor or even an established one who's not a star has to be is persistent. The rejections are behind you; concentrate on the future. It's the only sane and effective way."
—MORGAN FREEMAN (*Driving Miss Daisy*)

"Persist, then keep persisting. Maybe take a short break, then persist some more. A majority of new actors drop out before five years have passed. Those who hang in there five or more years have a far better chance of getting The Big Break than most newcomers."
—AARON ECKHART (*Love Happens*)

"If Best Actress Oscar winners like Kathy Bates and Jessica Tandy had quit during their first decade or two as actors, you'd never have heard of them. Acting is for the long run. You can't count on stardom— that's like winning the lottery. Success, though, is definitely attainable. It requires dedication, which means commitment and time and, sometimes, sacrifice." —KELLY MCGILLIS (*Top Gun*)

"Moms Mabley, the comedian, had an R-rated mouth before her time . . . when Redd Foxx came along, they called him the male Moms Mabley. Anyhow, she was on Johnny Carson's show when he asked, 'How does a lady get to be successful in a tough business like show business?' Moms said, 'Sometimes it involves not being a lady for a little while.'"
—HALLE BERRY

"Careers cannot be built on a casting couch. At most, it'll let you get your foot in the door. At worst, it'll ruin your reputation and make you a dirty joke."
—PHYLLIS DILLER

"Nowadays actors are also subject to the casting couch. I tell my students so; it's a reality. The difference is, a young man doesn't have to be degraded by it—he can just, as it were, lie back and enjoy it." —NINA FOCH, actor-coach

"I think most young people would like to be actors. But a lot of them don't think that they're attractive enough, which has little to do with acting. Or that they're not talented enough, which has little to do with Hollywood." —MICHAEL SHEEN (*Frost/Nixon*)

"Acting is something that most people think they're incapable of but they do it from morning to night." —MARLON BRANDO

"Adults think they're past and above make-believe, that acting's just for kids and actors. How self-deceiving that is!" —NANCY WALKER, actor-director

"Acting is when we put on an emotional mask. It's when we want something—whether it's in a scene or in real life—so we say the things and act the way we think we need to in order to achieve our objective." —JOSEPH GORDON-LEVITT (*Inception*)

"In ancient Greece . . . the old-fashioned moralists said the word for 'actor' and 'liar' was the same, because an actor pretends. So the old-fashioned moralists said act-

ing was bad, and tried to have it banned. But the audiences won, because actors not only entertain, they can occasionally give us insight and compassion and hope."
—MELINA MERCOURI, actress, member of the Greek Parliament, and a cabinet minister

"Acting is simply my way of investigating human nature and having fun at the same time." —MERYL STREEP

"Acting affords me the opportunity to behave in ways I never would in my own life." —HENRY FONDA

"I became an actor to meet chicks." —CHRIS PENN, Sean's younger brother

"Initially I got into acting to meet handsome actors." —Sir IAN MCKELLEN, aka "Gandalf"

"I grew up loving *The Wizard of Oz*. To tell you the truth, I longed to see the movie again and again because I wanted to go to Oz. I wanted to have a tornado sweep me up and take me away from the life I was living as a teenager. I wished that Auntie Em was my aunt." —JOHNNY DEPP

"You enter acting thinking you have talent, then find that's not enough. It has to be disciplined into a craft and you have to develop a technique to be able to draw on your talent repeatedly and under any given circumstance, at any sudden given moment. . . . The general public doesn't appreciate all that goes into a stage or screen performance. It's pretty awesome." —ALICIA SILVERSTONE (*Clueless*)

"I was the youngest brother [of four]. One reason I chose acting was so people would have to listen to me. When you say a line, people have to be quiet and hear you. That was important to me." —ERIC DOUGLAS, son of Kirk, brother of Michael

"Acting is all about listening. I think I listen a lot better as an actor than I do in real life." —SAM ROCKWELL (*Better Living Through Chemistry*)

"Film acting is talking softly and listening loud." —GEORGE STEVENS, director (*Giant*)

"Almost nobody likes their own voice. Even worse, when you hear it on tape. Don't let your voice throw you. Don't let others' opinion of your voice throw you. Actors' voices come in every conceivable sound and tone and pitch and accent and quirk. The mere fact that your voice is distinctive is a plus—it makes you more recognizable. And if your voice isn't special, neither are most actors' voices today, if you really listen to them." —BOB NEWHART

"You get close to finding out how you sound to others by cupping your ears and talking." —ERIC MORRIS, acting coach and author (*No Acting, Please*)

"In cinema's golden age, you only had to listen to a few words from a star and you knew who was speaking. Today it's mostly sound-alikes. The more people, and the farther we go into the population explosion, the more clone-like." —BEATRICE ARTHUR

"Before she became, posthumously, an icon and a goddess, Marilyn Monroe was criticized for you-name-it. Her voice, too. In her first several movies, she over-enunciated. Yet the way she did it was de-lightful. . . . People criticized her whispery voice. Well, that was the Marilyn sound! Sometimes it takes time for people to come to appreciate what is special." —JACK LEMMON, on his *Some Like It Hot* costar

"Hollywood is a place where they'll pay you a thousand dollars for a kiss and fifty cents for your soul. I know, because I turned down the first offer often enough, and held out for the fifty cents." —MARILYN MONROE

"People don't listen! They strictly judge from a stereotype. I keep reading that my voice is 'high-pitched.' That is patently, absurdly false. Listen to my voice! I may have a childlike speech pattern, possibly even babyish at times, but my voice is in fact not high-pitched. But one writer says it is, and then everyone latches on to that." —TRUMAN CAPOTE (*Murder by Death*)

"This mumbling thing I'm always accused of . . . I've done my share. The misperception is it's all I ever do, that it's my method. They call me a Method actor, but I did not learn from Lee Strasberg. I learned from Stella Adler. Yet people still write that Strasberg was my mentor, which is bullshit." —MARLON BRANDO

"For actors, the key is less what the voice sounds like than how it's used. In England, vocal training has been integral for aspiring actors. It gave us confidence and variety; hopefully it also makes us sound less boring." —VANESSA REDGRAVE, a graduate of London's Central School of Speech and Drama

"Why Hollywood overlooks the voice, I can't imagine. It must be that they think looks compensate for poor speech and voice patterns. That's hardly true even for sex symbols." —HELENA BONHAM CARTER (*The King's Speech*)

"New actors work on their look and sound, their technique. Lots of them need to work on their personalities. Because before becoming professionals, actors have to meet the hiring people and impress them. Being surly or sloppy, seeming needy or kooky, to list only four drawbacks, creates a lousy impression. Remember: first you interact, which boils down to auditioning and socializing, and then—if you get chosen—you act and get paid." —M. K. LEWIS, acting coach

"If you're truly ambitious and self-deluded enough, you may become desperate to someday be a star. That's your problem. But once you leave acting class for the real showbiz world, never let your desperate ambition show. It will lose you the job every time." —PETER BULL, British character actor

"Those in charge of jobs want reliable people. In front of them, you must play it cool. Never admit you're dying for that job or role—that makes them nervous. It scares them off." —PEGGY FEURY, acting coach

"You can be extremely talented, but avoid extremes of attitude. Don't pretend apathy about a job you really want to book, but don't be arrogant, as if you're dead-sure you'll get it. Best bet is to act realistically, casually optimistic." —JOHN FRANKENHEIMER, director (*Birdman of Alcatraz*)

"You can greatly improve your chances to get hired if, apart from talent, you seem a nice, dependable person. Nobody wants to work with a creep, unless he's a guaranteed major moneymaker." —WALTER LOTT, acting coach

"We've all watched TV and wondered about a certain performer in some older motion picture what ever happened to him and why, since he seemed to have it all, he never became a big star? The two biggest factors: one,

he didn't appear in enough hit movies; two, he crossed too many people and trashed his opportunities."
—GARSON KANIN, filmmaker

"We knew a gorgeous gal who was convinced her glamorous allure was her ticket to Hollywood. She was very photogenic and became a leading model. But a leading lady? See, to be an actor means to *act*. To perform action. To know how to initiate and sustain motion. To speak lines—as if for the first time. To create an emotion and then be able to duplicate it, take after take.

"This was all beyond our pampered, not very active—I guess one would say 'proactive' now—friend. So at 30 her modeling career was over. She married a guy who before she hit 40 dumped her for a younger model, I mean a younger woman."
—BRADFORD DILLMAN, actor married to model Suzy Parker, who had a brief acting career

"Energy is probably any performer's best friend. Not the sort of chemically induced energy that eventually did poor Judy Garland in, which MGM initially fed her without her knowledge, like putting Benzedrine in her soup, but the energy that comes from a healthy lifestyle and diet and lots and lots and lots of self-belief!" —ANN MILLER, actress-dancer

"Whether people are praising or panning your acting, you ought to take both with a big grain of salt. The one

opinion that counts in the long run is your own. You must believe you're a big enough talent and a worthy enough person that all those rejections only get you down temporarily. Nothing must get you down to the point that you don't, within a day or two, maximum, bounce right back up and try all over again."
—FELICITY HUFFMAN (*Desperate Housewives*)

"To be an actor is to be perennially seeking the next job. Most actors' time isn't spent acting, it's spent looking for the chance to act, sometimes even for no money."
—CAMPBELL SCOTT (*The Dying Gaul*)

"Talent, sure . . . some. But personality and looks count for more. Or personality for a character actor. But having tremendous reserves of energy and persistence counts for even more than looks and personality."
—DANIEL J. TRAVANTI (*Hill Street Blues*)

"If you can't take rejection, don't become a writer . . . or any other type of artist, and especially not an actor. Rejection is practically their whole way of life." —GORE VIDAL, writer who occasionally acted in films

"The public, via the media, hears or reads about the highs of acting. The relatively few highs. That's like one small lane of highs, compared to an eight-lane, eight-mile boulevard of lows and no's that the media chooses not to spotlight." —FARRAH FAWCETT

"When you finally attain some success in acting, there's always somebody more successful to remind you—they'll actually tell you—that it's not such a big deal. It is, though, a big, threatening deal to most of your non-actor friends, and sooner or later you'll lose them. Behind your back they'll say you've gotten too big for your britches. Even if you've barely changed. Maybe you've just gotten too big for *their* britches."
—JOAN RIVERS

"I was an actor for a time—I acted with Marilyn Monroe, so that's something. But I'm glad I'm not an actor any more. Actors, like beautiful women, can never be sure if they're liked for themselves or for what shows, like good looks or success. You have to keep doubting people's sincerity, and frankly that's rather tiresome and depressing."
—JACK PAAR, former *Tonight Show* host

"When I won my Oscar [for *West Side Story*] and went backstage, Joan Crawford was all over me, showering me with smiles and congratulations. She seemed so happy for me! She gave every indication we were becoming best friends for life. Later I realized she was 'happy' for every Academy Award winner—and posing for photos with as many of them as she could." —RITA MORENO

"Trust and keep the friends you make before you're famous. The ones who boost you and give you confidence when no one else does, even your own mother. Like Marty Erlichman . . . all these decades, he and Barbra have done business together on a long-ago handshake; they've never signed a contract." —ELLIOTT GOULD, Streisand's first husband, on the singer's longtime manager

"Parents are more concerned with security than dreams. So they tend to discourage their kids away from showbiz. If it were up to parents, there'd probably be no stars. Our mother wanted Barbra to find employment with the school system, for security and a good pension. She didn't see that much in her." —ROSLYN KIND, singer and Streisand's half-sister

"For an actor, it helps a lot if you're your own secret #1 fan." —PAUL GIAMATTI (*Sideways*)

"Nobody is glamorous to the people they live with. You need a strong sense of your own uniqueness before you can go out and try to claim your spot in the showbiz firmament." —LORRAINE BRACCO (*The Sopranos*)

"You have, like, this general idea floating around your head about your personal identity. That can get so shaken up when you start meeting acting teachers and casting people, etc., 'cause they'll tell you exactly how they perceive you. It's disorienting, but it's useful, because you're going to get cast not based on your own perceptions but on how the powers that be define you." —STEVE CARELL (*The Way, Way Back*)

"Somebody may think he's the next great James Bond villain, but then he gets cast as the dorky neighbor in some TV sitcom. . . . Actors don't generally get to choose which medium they work in, nor the genre they're slotted into, nor specific roles or types. That is what casting is for." —DODIE MCLEAN, casting director

"Individual actors are basically powerless. The hiring entities exert a sweeping control over most actors. It could be worse . . . thank goodness for the Screen Actors Guild!" —PATTY DUKE, former SAG president

"It's unsettling, to say the least, when you think you're good-looking and everyone is pointing you toward comedy." —ELLEN DEGENERES

"I thought of myself in potential terms of a great tragedienne, given my family history and personal inclinations. But I wasn't ethereal or slim enough . . . perhaps not graceful enough, and then I broke through with *Georgy Girl* . . . then had to battle the stereotyping and weight situations to become 'The Happy Hooker.' That wasn't how I saw myself, either, but at least it was a drastic change!" —LYNN REDGRAVE

"Laurence [Fishburne] thinks he's devastatingly sexy and all, but most of my girlfriends think he's cute and kind of goofy." —ANGELA BASSETT (*What's Love Got to Do with It*)

"I have a great sense of humor, but I'm not one to smile aimlessly. Doesn't mean I'm angry. But even before [James] Bond, I was seldom cast in any comedies. I got a lot of grim roles. Still do." —DANIEL CRAIG

"If you're an actress and overweight, that immediately pigeonholes you. Into supporting roles, into comedy. It's something we need to change, seeing as how the average American is now obese. Like they've long said, fat is a feminist issue." —MELISSA MCCARTHY (*The Heat*)

"Entertainment is part of your leisure time. You're supposed to enjoy what you see and hear. I wouldn't get up in front of an audience not looking my best. I do comedy, but people want me to look nice. I want me to look nice. If you want to look like a bus, park yourself in a barn!" —JUDY TENUTA, comedienne-actress

"What Hollywood, U.S.A., needs to do is recognize that there are minorities, plural. Like, where are East Asians on TV? I was the first [in her short-lived series *All-American Girl*] and didn't think I'd be one of the last. I'm Korean, but, hello, China has the world's biggest population, except you'd never know it according to Hollywood." —MARGARET CHO

"Females, half or more of the population, are a minority on big and little screens, while older women are an endangered species. I think Hollywood is appalling." —JANE FONDA

"For a long time on television, you saw more characters from outer space than of Hispanic origin. Now we're the #1 minority, but far from it in terms of media visibility." —EDWARD JAMES OLMOS

"Dark-skinned actresses have confided to me how often they encounter a skewed and sexist brand of racism. A movie's leading man can be literally black, but his romantic interest—the wife or girlfriend—has to be several shades lighter. This often results in hiring a biracial actress, leaving the dark actress out in the cold." —MILTON KATSELAS, director-coach

"There is a peculiarly American marketing practice where they hire an actress or a singer who is half black and half white, then they pass her off as 'black.' Instead of being herself, she is made to misrepresent one group. It's political, but it's also about selling. It's also because America is a polarized nation." —ALAIN RESNAIS, French director

"I had one c.d. [casting director] tell me I wasn't 'right' for a role as this movie star's lover. No explanation— she didn't admit I wasn't much lighter-skinned than he was . . . and they ended up with an actress way lighter than me! But now I'm playing a vampire queen with a beautiful white male lover, and nobody's measuring who's pale enough." —AALIYAH (*Queen of the Damned*)

"It's harder to be yourself in go-see's and meetings if you're gay. It's still the one minority status most actors are supposed to, even encouraged, to hide." —NEIL PATRICK HARRIS

"So much of acting is lying or pretending that it's quite easy to stay in the closet while you're establishing yourself. It's later, after you've made it, that you can contemplate coming out. If you come out too soon, no one might ever hear about you. Isn't that just so backward?" —T. R. KNIGHT (*Grey's Anatomy*)

"Larry [Olivier] had a mania for losing himself in a role. He loved false noses and disguises. He enjoyed assorted accents. My own voice and persona have been more fixed, and I tend to be visible in my characters. Largely by choice." —Sir JOHN GIELGUD

"I can't tell you why we choose things. I wanted to be a doctor and my [identical] twin sister wanted to be an actress. On vacation, we went to Chicago to see my brother perform in the chorus of a show, which was very exciting—to me, anyway—and when we returned home she'd given up her desire to act and I gave up studying medicine for acting." —ANN B. DAVIS (Alice on *The Brady Bunch*)

"I played the comic, bumbling sidekick on *I Dream of Jeannie*, which locked me into that niche, and then I was the comic, bumbling neighbor on *The Bob Newhart Show*, and that was that. If you do a thing well, you get rewarded for it and stuck with it." —BILL DAILY

"Before *Gilligan's Island* I did a slew of different characters, though not usually villains. But I always envied my father's wide-ranging career. He played everything, and often. . . . After a few seasons of *Gilligan*, nobody could see me as anything but Skipper, and there weren't any more 'Skipper' roles, so I opened a restaurant instead." —ALAN HALE, JR.

"Being on a very popular TV series can be the kiss of death for your career. In the movies I was Charlie Chan's #2 son, but I could also enact a semi-villain, as in *The Letter* with Bette Davis. But when *Bonanza* came along, I had the tiny role of the cook, Hop Sing . . . a jokey stereotype. That part erased my credibility and the memory of my numerous roles in the movies.

"And, as has often been said, I was the only regular

on *Bonanza* who did not become a millionaire."
—VICTOR SEN YUNG

"[The TV series] *My Three Sons* made me a fortune, but it pretty well put paid to my career in motion pictures. I think weekly familiarity breeds a sort of contempt."
—FRED MACMURRAY

"Over lo these many decades I've played my share of tough ladies and broads. But *Golden Girls* was so popular in first-run and reruns that now I have to put my foot down hard if I want to play a bitch. Bitches are fun, and believe me, I'm no Rose Nyland!"
—BETTY WHITE

"Is it easier to play anger than compassion? Completely depends on the sort of individual you are."
—RUTGER HAUER, Dutch actor (*Spetters*)

"Some emotions are less accessible, say, to men. Such as vulnerability and crying. Contrarily, some actresses find it uncomfortable or impossible to play hard-as-nails, and so they don't. Or they don't until they're older and get cast that way." —Dame JUDI DENCH

"In our minds, we're younger than we really are. Still, it can jolt an actress when she remembers the sweet young things she used to play and then realizes that past 35 or 40 all she's being offered are harridans and black-hearted harpies." —UTA HAGEN, actress-coach who played Martha in *Who's Afraid of Virginia Woolf?* on Broadway

"I don't regret doing it at all. Why should I? If I regret anything, it's Hollywood trying to villain-ize feminine characters as an actress matures." —ELIZABETH TAYLOR, Martha in the film version of *Who's Afraid of Virginia Woolf?*, on her second Oscar-winning role

"It's disgusting how often a Latina character is still named Maria, lives in a ghetto, and has a problem son. Still the stereotyping. . . . The only solution is for more young Hispanics to consider writing or directing, instead of always wanting to act or sing. When you act or sing, you are employed to deliver what somebody else has already written." —KATY JURADO (*High Noon*)

"The writer gets minimal respect in Hollywood. Even so, the guys who write the movies and [TV] programs have the power of creation, and that influences everything you see and more of what you think than you think." —NORMAN MAILER

"You hear about writers wanting to become directors, a natural enough transition. But writers and actors, they're supposed to be like oil and water. Fact of the matter is, I can write. I'm a writer too. I don't advertise the fact, but it does come in handy . . . if I'm saddled with inane dialogue, I just rewrite it." —ROBERT MITCHUM

"I put my guts into a script I knew would sell. But I'd only sell it if the studio put it in the contract that I got to play Rocky Balboa. It was my way of breaking into acting, big-time." —SYLVESTER STALLONE

"The actor is an athlete of the heart." —ANTONIN ARTAUD, French playwright

"We're ordinary people with extraordinary jobs." —JULIA ROBERTS

"What fascinates me is looking at photos of stars when they were kids or teens, or even in their early twenties. Many did not seem very special. Not stunning, not that distinctive. . . . Marilyn Monroe, Sophia Loren, a bunch of them. But what they became by the time they were 30! Wow. Being in the limelight must have strong transformative powers." —KENN DUNCAN, photographer

"During the movies' golden age, diets were forced on plump newcomers like Greta Garbo, the rotten teeth of a Joan Crawford were fixed, a Clark Gable got fitted with decent dentures, Rita Hayworth underwent electrolysis, and so forth. They turned sows' ears into silk purses. 'They' being a small army of hairdressers, makeup artists, dentists, and other physical technicians." —DOUGLAS WHITNEY, film historian

"I don't think anyone is born an actor. Still, little children who play 'pretend' more often and perhaps better than other children are probably more inclined to enter the acting profession." —DIANE KRUGER (*Inglourious Basterds*)

"Acting is the most minor of gifts and not a very high-class way to earn a living. After all, Shirley Temple could do it at the age of four." —KATHARINE HEPBURN

"It may be the lost kingdom of childhood I am in constant search for." —LIV ULLMANN

"The old cliché has a lot of truth in it: that many or most actors got very little attention, and maybe not very much love, as kids, so they seek for both as adults." —Dr. JOYCE BROTHERS, psychologist

"I've known actors who had dull, bland, ordinary parents and maybe wanted a more colorful future for themselves. On the other hand, I've known actors who had quite memorable, colorful parents that maybe they wanted to top. . . . Who can guess what mental currents lead somebody to choose acting?" —STAN KAMEN, William Morris agent

"My mother's way larger than life. We'd have nightly gatherings around the dinner table that usually ended in a harangue by my mother, in truly Wagnerian volume. She'd rail against whomever was the Republican president at the time, blaming him for this or that social injustice. An opera-singing father and a mother who could really make herself heard when she got up on her soapbox—I guess that's how I learned to project my voice on stage." —KEVIN KLINE (*In & Out*)

"When I was about eight I got bullied on the school bus by a boy who kept stealing my Twinkies. So I dressed up as my big brother, slicked my hair back, put on his shades and boots, along with a lot of attitude and swagger, and tried to pass myself off as Nicky Coppola's brother Richard, and told him I was going to kick him right up his ass.

"Nobody stole my Twinkies again." —NICOLAS CAGE, Oscar winner and director, Francis Ford Coppola's nephew

"In Japan, shyness is considered a positive trait. Not in North America, where being a boy and shy is a social liability. Being a shy boy who's polite is worse—people abuse that kind of decency. But nowhere more so than in Hollywood, where toughness is the standard. Even for most actresses.

"An actor looking to be a leading man is required to be tough and aggressive. Obnoxious is okay too.

Hollywood has a long history of obnoxious leading men." —SCOTT THOMPSON, Canadian, of *The Kids in the Hall*

"Almost every gay man is a good actor by the time he's a teen. We have to pretend to be what we're not, because the vast majority of us grow up in all-hetero households. We typically have to hide our emotional and sexual nature from even our parents and siblings. So of course we're good actors! Until recently, we had no choice."—PATRICK BRISTOW (*Ellen*)

"Tomboys are given leeway as long as they eventually get a boyfriend or state an interest in boys. But those gay boys who are noticeably gay get no leeway, and either have to live like undercover spies or suffer the consequences. . . . If they're handsome and can 'pass,' they sometimes go into acting, which is more make-believe, but it pays very nicely." — DALE OLSON, publicist and an associate of Rock Hudson

"It strikes me as perverse that actresses must be fresh, vulnerable, and innocent on screen in spite of having to wise up and toughen up to stay in the game and win at it. Hollywood can be truly destructive for women. . . . If you're beautiful and have the sensitivity of a rhinoceros, you've got a chance there." —STELLA STEVENS (*A Town Called Bastard*)

"If you're sensitive, run, don't walk, away from Tinseltown. I was hired as bait by Fox to get Marilyn Monroe to return to work. Even then, I sensed she was on a collision course with life, after all the struggles, insecurities, and indignities she endured in Hollywood." —SHEREE NORTH (*How to Be Very, Very Popular*)

"Men will come on to you as an actress. It happens a lot, in one form or another. Fear of sexual harassment can be a deterrent, but the point is, an actress has to firmly say no. In a nonthreatening, semi-friendly way. You don't want to make enemies. But you don't dare to get a sleazy reputation." —EVA MENDES (*The Women*)

"If you're female and a genuine talent, whether comedic or singing, whatever, but not a sexy beauty, count your blessings. You can have a longer career than the sexpot, and you won't have to fend lecherous men off at every turn." —PAULA POUNDSTONE, comedian

"As an actress, I feel that my identity is for rent. Not for sale, but for rent." —ANNA DEAVERE SMITH (*Rent*)

"To completely become an artist is to expose yourself. You can't say, 'Don't look at me, I'm exposing myself.'" —DANIEL CRAIG

"Acting is standing up naked and turning around very slowly." —ROSALIND RUSSELL (*Auntie Mame*)

"I'm not a performer. I don't want to hop up on a stage and go, 'Look at me! I'm Renee! What do you think?' That's not me. What I do is very different. If I want to express something, it's through the filter [of a character]. So I never feel exposed." —RENEE ZELLWEGER

"I have such a fear of embarrassing myself that I will do anything not to embarrass myself. That's it. That's the key to my success." —MICHELLE PFEIFFER

"Don't be shy about introducing yourself to crew members. If you do get embarrassed, pick one: the editor. He might do more for you and your performance than anyone else because he can choose or influence how much of your performance goes into the finished project." —ALEXANDER GOLITZEN, art director (*Spartacus*)

"At the end of a take, don't go dead when the director yells, 'Cut!' Keep acting with your face, subtly yet expressively. Use your eyes or mouth, your cheek muscles—if you don't know you have cheek muscles, you haven't been acting, you've been reciting. Chances are, editors will leave more of you in, at least in the rough cut. You can't usually be in the final cut if you're not in the rough cut.

"That little extra is called a 'button.' Directors and editors like buttons, to transition into the next scene."
—MICKEY GROSSMAN, Chicago agent

"A sparkly, sizeable chunk of success in our business is recognizing your opportunities and taking them. Don't be afraid, don't over-hesitate. 'Why not?' typically works better than, 'Oh, I shouldn't.'" —SUE MENGERS, Barbra Streisand's agent

"It's not just that people recognize you in public once you're a celebrity. That, I can handle—it's like going back to a little hometown where many people know you. What's embarrassing is the things some people say to your face. They think you're impervious to personal comments and criticism. 'You've gained weight, haven't you?' 'They must use a lot of makeup to improve your complexion.' Or 'What do they do to hide the wrinkles?' It's incredible!" —BETTY GARRETT (*Laverne and Shirley*)

"The worst is when they recognize you and get embarrassed because they don't know your name. They'll never ask it. They'll either ask if you're somebody else or they'll waste their time and yours trying to come up with your name. Usually at most they'll come up with *one* of your names."
—RICHARD DEACON (*The Dick Van Dyke Show*)

"I've seen homeless people ask someone for a quarter,

then when I pass by they ask for a dollar, and if I don't give it, they sometimes yell and curse me!" —TONY RANDALL (*The Odd Couple*)

"If people find out I have a famous sister, a lot of them want to meet her. Some have tried to make friends with me so they can meet and make friends with her. If I say I can't introduce them, some get angry, even abusive. I'm proud of my sister, but her fame could intrude on my life big-time if I let it." —RICHARD TOMLIN, Lily's younger brother

"If I do an interview, which I almost never do, do you think the interviewer could ever possibly not ask about my mother?" —JASON GOULD (*Prince of Tides*), son of Barbra Streisand and Elliott Gould

"A sadly negative aspect of fame is being exploited. A contractor or a car mechanic will try and charge you double. Or someone tries to take your photo unaware—especially from an unflattering angle— to sell to a tabloid. And so on and so forth. It can make you leery of going out in public." —KRISTIN CHENOWETH (*Running with Scissors*)

"Soon after he opened Disneyland, Walt Disney invited me and my kids to his house, where he had a life-sized railroad system. He told the boys to call him 'Uncle Walt,' and I was surprised when he filmed them riding his trains—filmed the whole thing. A few weeks later, there was my family on his TV show. 'Uncle Walt' had filmed me and my kids as a big commercial for his new amusement park. Without telling me.

"My business manager insisted that I sue him, so I did. Then my wife Anne said, 'Are you crazy?' Even if you win, you lose—everybody loves Walt Disney.' I dropped the suit." —KIRK DOUGLAS

"In Hollywood, friendship takes a back seat. Barbra Streisand and Sue Mengers, her agent, were friends. Mengers's husband was directing a movie. The leading lady was fired, so Mengers got Streisand to replace her, for $4 million. Sue sent Barbra a check for $3.6 million—agents always send actors their checks, minus their own ten-percent commission. Barbra fired Sue. She thought she'd done her a favor by stepping into her husband's movie. Sue hadn't seen it that way, in view of the four mil.

"Most of Hollywood's beautiful friendships are up on the screen." —JOHN ALONZO, cinematographer (*Chinatown*)

"Some celebrities socialize [together]. Most don't . . . there's conscious or unconscious competition. Who's the bigger star? All I know is, when I'm invited to Sidney Poitier's house, I'm supposed to feel very honored. We both come from the [Caribbean] islands. But that was long ago. . . ." —HARRY BELAFONTE, singer-actor

"When I worked in Hollywood I got the double impression that people admired and looked up to me and that they resented and looked down on me. Some individuals there are delightful, but all in all there is tremendous hidden aggression and insincerity. I never really felt at home there." —Sir JOHN GIELGUD (*Arthur*)

"The Scottish actor David McCallum's role was originally an occasional one, but the producers made us into a duo . . . the result was that *The Man From U.N.C.L.E.* zoomed in popularity. David, a real gentleman, always let me stand on his right, traditionally considered the more prominent position, when we did publicity—and we did a whole lot of publicity!" —ROBERT VAUGHN

"You learn early in Hollywood to hide your agenda. If you can't stand someone but they can further your career, you're nice to them. That sort of thing. Which helps with acting, because a lot of it revolves around saying or promising one thing but intending another. Sooner or later all actors have to play that." —WANDA SYKES (*Monster-in-Law*)

"Most people think acting is about what you show. You know, on your face, in your gestures . . . about what you reveal. But think about it: half the time, in plays and movies, a character will cover up what she really wants or feels. As, often, in real life. . . .

That is subtext, and for actors it's often as important as the text itself." —OLYMPIA DUKAKIS, Oscar winner

"Dialogue is what a character is willing to reveal, willing to share with another person. The 90 percent he or she isn't willing to share is what I do for a living." —MARTIN LANDAU (*Ed Wood*)

"A crying scene is more realistic and touches an audience more if your character tries to hide that she's crying, if she denies that she's crying, if she's trying hard not to cry. Flat-out crying, sobbing, or weeping—all that's a turnoff. It's what children do, not what adults do." —GLENN CLOSE

"Never indicate. People don't try to show their feelings. They try to hide them." —ROBERT DE NIRO

"If you look at silent movies, you'll see actors indicating emotions and reactions like mad. Okay, maybe they had to—they didn't have sound then. But today there's no excuse for such hamminess." —JAKE GYLLENHAAL (*Brokeback Mountain*)

"It used to be that audiences loved getting what they expected from actors—from stars, I should say. You never got much emotional range from John Wayne, and Henry Fonda was always a well-mannered good guy. Audiences even accepted the hammy theatrics of John Barrymore—they called it style. We wouldn't call it that today. "Today we expect realism and a bit more versatility. Today you're not supposed to become your own stereotype." —WYATT COOPER, movie critic and Anderson's father

"A famous actress I'll refrain from naming once admitted to me during a costume fitting that she, like many of her sisterhood, had been interested in exploring character as a young actress. But as an older actress and an above-the-title star, the character she was most interested in exploring was her own." —WALTER PLUNKETT, designer (*Gone with the Wind*)

"Not being a superstar myself, and I'm half relieved not to be, I can speculate that stars become hard and imperious due to the demands and strain of staying on top, and to the criticism and jealousy hurled at them from every side once they've reached the top." —ROSE MARIE (*The Dick Van Dyke Show*)

"Some actors wind up more hardened than others . . . an underprivileged childhood, an abusive parent? But people are people, and when I hear about a man's 'feminine side,' I cringe. Because that'll scare most men off. Just say their softer or vulnerable side. Everybody has one. And as an actor you have to be able to access most or all of your sides." —FREDERICK COMBS, actor-coach

"I'm not one for this labeling of emotions as belonging to one gender or the other. It divides actors and actresses too much. It can separate half of us from what are human feelings, feelings common to all human beings." —DELPHINE BOURGAULT, acting coach

"It is an old-fashioned business. We still say 'actress.' But we no longer say poetess, stewardess, manageress, laundress, sculptress, authoress, or aviatrix. And 'leading lady.' Did we ever have a 'leading gentleman'? And where are the leading women?" —VALERIE HARPER

"Once I became a star, I had the luxury to [be able to] say no to scripts about a silly girl fooled by the opposite sex. I could choose to play someone closer to my personality. Of course my films always involved love and sex. . . . In my own life, it is I who leaves the man. I choose, and I decide. When it ends, I am the one to leave." —BRIGITTE BARDOT, French sex symbol who retired at 40

"Actors may be more marketable when they're young and bed-able, but they get better with age because the longer you live, the more ideas you have. And accumulated ideas give an actor power. . . . No actor can be as good at 20 or 30 as at 50 or 60. Time. Ideas. Experience." —STELLA ADLER, acting guru

"What's invigorating about acting is the newness of

each new gig, a new character, new people to work with. Most jobs fall into a sameness of routine, surroundings, personnel. But after decades in the biz, it's always something new and fresh. It doesn't get stale. It just gets harder to book a new job." —JOEY BISHOP, Rat Pack member

"I no longer get the girl, but I get the part."
—MICHAEL CAINE

"I still get as nervous as a virgin when I start a new role. I give as much to a part as ever. The feeling is still exciting, and in the part I feel that I am exciting. If I'm not, please don't tell me. Let me keep my illusion." —ROD STEIGER

"People get into show business to continue having fun. I always told our cast that we were there to have fun, then to entertain the 300 people in the live audience, and then to transport it out to the audience at home. It was about fun." —CAROL BURNETT

"Acting is about giving. Often, you feel like you'd act in a certain project for free. . . . Mostly, it's about giving of your knowledge, your feelings, sharing your essence. Yes, they're somebody else's lines, but they come through the vessel of you. Every Hamlet speaks Shakespeare's lines, but every Hamlet is different. Each Hamlet is *that* actor." —Sir DEREK JACOBI (*I, Claudius*)

"Actors are the best people in the movie business. They're the ones willing to put the most on the line. I feel this more when I'm directing. It's the toughest job in the business. You have to create a world inside your own experience and hold on to it while they're putting up lights and fluffing pillows and all that stuff. I think there's a real generous spirit at the heart of that."
—SEAN PENN, two-time Oscar winner

"There are three kinds of actors. There's the actor who acts for himself, there's the actor who acts for the audience, and the actor who acts for the other actors. The actor who acts for the other actors is the only one who's an actor. . . . The one who acts for the audience is at least doing it for someone, and the one who's doing it for himself is not an actor." —MICHAEL CHEKHOV, acting guru

"No notices, however good, can ever quite satisfy an actor. No applause is ever quite long enough. At the end of a reception, no matter how tumultuous, one part of an actor's vanity must ask, 'Yes, but why have you stopped?'" —Sir MICHAEL REDGRAVE

"Acting provides the fulfillment of never being fulfilled. You're never as good as you'd like to be. So there's always something to hope for." —GLENDA JACKSON, two-time Oscar winner

"Love yourself in art, not art in yourself."
—KONSTANTIN STANISLAVSKY

2

AUDITIONING

"All you have to remember is 'audition' is synonymous with 'opportunity.' I mean, if you absolutely hate auditions, do you also hate opportunities? That wouldn't make much sense." —HILARY SWANK, two-time Oscar winner

"You can hate auditions, but that's a mindset, and it won't help you. It might not hurt you, but a positive mindset about auditions will help you. Hating or loving something is a choice. For your own sake, why not choose positively?" —JESSICA ALBA

"Actors will complain endlessly about auditioning. Don't bother. It's not gonna change, and we've heard it all before. And yes, it's tough. So's life. Besides, anything worth as much as success in show business is very tough to achieve. It can be done, but of *course*

it's not easy—otherwise everyone would be a star."
—JOSEPH STEFANO, screenwriter (*Psycho*)

"How often we see an actor come in with that look of I'd-rather-be-anyplace-else. Most try to hide it, some don't bother. My own reaction to such a look is: why aren't you someplace else?" —GERMAINE BOUCHARD, Canadian casting director

"You're being judged as an actor and a personality from the moment you walk in. Of course have a good walk, be aware of your body language and posture, but the eyes . . . number one is the eyes. No matter your personal problems or lack of sleep or whatever, alert eyes! Eyes full of life and curiosity. Eyes that acknowledge other people and are ready to take direction—and to get hired!" —WILLIAM BELASCO, agent

"Eyes can be used to seduce. The truth is, most of us want to be seduced, one way or another. Stars can seduce both sexes with their eyes." —ED LIMATO, agent of Richard Gere and Madonna

"The focused eye is paramount in an audition. If you concentrate on the here and now, your eye won't be distracted and wander. Make strong eye contact . . . more importantly, when reading, and especially if you're reading to the wall or into the distance, your eye must focus on a point where we believe the other person is. If it's not focused, we know you're just saying lines." —JOE WIZAN, former William Morris agent

"Most actors know that in a headshot the most important factor is the eyes. Yet during a general meeting or audition so many forget about the eyes and that we need to see their eyes! They look down at the floor or their hands or bury their faces in the sides . . . anything so we can't see the life in their eyes. Or whether there is any." —ROBERT WHITEHEAD, Broadway producer (*Master Class*)

"We'd rather you stumble through your lines than have you say them smoothly off your script but keep your eyes hidden or hooded. . . . Even more than your voice, your eyes are the leading aspect of your acting and your eligibility."—JADIN WONG, agent

"This actress came in . . . intelligent, attractive in an unusual way. You could tell she'd stand up for herself. When she read with other actors—we called her back—she didn't just look at them, she appraised them. She'd stare, but not too long, and evaluate a person or a statement, then make a decision that she kept to herself. Very interesting performer. You wanted to know more. . . ." —PAT BROOKS, casting director

"I did two things that helped get me that plum role

[opposite Joan Crawford in *Sudden Fear*]. I was polite. She may or may not have been a lady, but she expected to be treated as one. I heard she'd wanted Brando for the role [a younger husband], but he sent back word he wasn't interested in 'mother-son' projects.

"The other thing, knowing the strength and force of the character I wanted to play, is I channeled my emotion into and through my eyes. I stared, I kept from blinking—which is not very comfortable after several seconds . . . I used my eyes like weapons. I got that role, and my piercing stare or glare was instrumental." —JACK PALANCE, who won an Oscar for *City Slickers*

"There is no such thing as 'breaks.' If you're looking for 'breaks' you've got your eye on the wrong thing. Many people turn down opportunities because they're usually disguised as hard work. You'd be amazed the people who won't go out on a limb or progress or change and hurt a little for a while, to expand their powers. Most are prone to take the easy way, the comfy way.

"If you're not hurting a little, you're not growing." —PHYLLIS DILLER

"There is less courtesy than there used to be, maybe because there's less time. One used to get more time with a casting agent or director. Now, in addition to being hurried, some are actually rude. That's a challenge to any actor, not to get your feelings hurt and not to snap back at Mr. or Ms. Needlessly Rude.

"There is no excuse for rudeness, but it does happen. You just have to ignore it, which by doing so, you might leave behind a very favorable impression." —DORIS ROBERTS (*Hester Street*)

"Not to condescend, but a little thought that helps me through auditions is about those people behind the table: Can they do any better than I'm going to, than I am doing? If they could, I don't think they'd be behind that table right now. . . ." —BRAD DAVIS (*Midnight Express*)

"The fact of the matter is that the overwhelming majority of actors are smarter than the overwhelming majority of the people who are interviewing." —RICHARD DREYFUSS

"Very few actors are consistently, foolishly optimistic. This is not a business for optimism, any more than gambling is, although the odds are better than in gambling. . . . After you exit an audition, instead of feeling down or negative, just think and say to yourself, 'Next time, I'll fail better.'" —ROBERT REED (*The Brady Bunch*)

"Did you 'fail' at an audition? Not really. Of the, say, 50 people there, only one got to win. But the rest of you didn't fail, because you tried. And what you didn't get this time, you might get next time, from the same casting people. No, the only ones who failed are the ones who weren't at the audition." —RUTH WEBB, agent

"A very funny actor, good-looking too, read for a national ad. Everyone loved him except the sponsor. The actor failed to book the job because he just barely mispronounced the product's name. Twice." —LESLIE SCOTT, commercial agent

"One, commercials are a huge percentage of the total work that actors get. Two, and therefore, don't look down your nose at them unless you're a movie star, in which case you'll do them sooner or later anyway. Three, they are not as easy as they look. Four, never ever look down your nose at the product." — WILLIAM SCHALLERT, former Screen Actors Guild president

"When I did that takeoff on the old actor auditioning to sell potato chips—Frumpy's, or something like that—it was a fantasy and a hoot. In reality, they wouldn't have tolerated him for two minutes, he was so unaware of the product. To sell a product, whatever it may be, you've got to believe in it. Even pretend it's your religion, if that's what it takes. Acting is what it takes." —WALTER MATTHAU, recalling *The Sunshine Boys*

"Embarrassed to fall in love with a laundry detergent? Don't go out for commercial auditions. You have to pitch it. You gotta love it. You gotta want to share it with everyone!" —JOANNE WORLEY (*Rowan & Martin's Laugh-In*)

"For me, the key to success in commercials is you've discovered a product so good that you want to tell your best friend about it, like doing her a favor. And the camera is the best friend you tell it to. That's pretty much it." —SANDY DUNCAN (*Star Spangled Girl*)

"Guys, don't be afraid to show your goofy side . . . to be more than a strong and silent lump. Sometimes it's the high-pitched laugh—like Tom Selleck had—or a softer side that gets you the part. Unless you're the lead in a Western, be emotionally creative; the casting people love it. Don't hide your feminine side—everyone has one, even a Lithuanian lesbian that I know." —JIM J. BULLOCK (*Alf*)

"Extremes of masculinity and femininity aren't really natural, they're poses. A certain degree of vulnerability and ambiguity in either gender creates audience interest. The extremes are too cardboard." —LEE MARVIN (*Cat Ballou*)

"It's less than before, but females may still use a higher, wispier voice in front of men, to seem more feminine. I know some who use a deeper, more naturally interesting voice in their work than in everyday life.

"It's not so much about being heard, 'cause

everyone can be miked now. It's a question of being taken seriously. A Marilyn Monroe voice hampered her career way back then. Today, unless it was Marilyn Monroe herself, it would be an unacceptable, politically incorrect joke." —NANCY WALKER, actor-director

"You'll hear, if you watch her body of work—no pun intended—that Marilyn didn't always talk like *that*, like in our movie. She had a more realistic voice. But the breathy little-girl sound was what the producers kept dragging her back to. As she got older, it seemed less right. Less dignified. Marilyn was too vulnerable to the judgments of others. She never developed that necessary hard core." —TOM EWELL, Monroe's costar in *The Seven Year Itch*

"Actors should remember what Eleanor Roosevelt said, that nobody can be made to feel inferior without their consent. Presentation and confidence are everything. Shyness appeals professionally only in very young girls. You may feel nervous or hesitant, but you must appear erect, vigorous, intelligent, and determined. Not obnoxious, but proud of yourself and glad to be meeting the bigwig. Don't slouch in, don't mumble, do look the other party in the eye and smile, but not constantly." —JANE FEINBERG, casting director

"It's often and usually forgotten that, apart from

age, the biggest differentiation between a 'star' actor and a supporting actor is posture." —FREDERICK COMBS, actor-coach (the play and the movie of *The Boys in the Band*)

"She had perfect posture, but it was rather intimidating. She looked as if she'd swallowed a yardstick." —GLENN FORD, on Joan Crawford

"He would plant himself, out there on location, as if he was a tower or a steeple defying any strong wind to knock him down." —JOAN HACKETT, on costar Charlton Heston

"You have to know your type. Arrogance usually works best on a star, a female European. But it varies. . . . This joke was going around town after Faye Dunaway had passed her peak and a c.d. met her at a party and she didn't act as big-shot and aloof as he'd assumed she would. But as he put it, 'Half aloof is better than none.'" —FRAN BASCOM, casting director

"Actors are informed often enough that they must look like their headshots. What's off-putting or occasionally funny but not professionally smart is when their manner and movement—their voice too—doesn't match the photo. I've seen glamour gals bustle in, with a confidential manner, eager to please, no mystery, no glamour at all. So why did they choose that headshot? Did the photographer talk them into it or hyp-

notize them? Be what your photo conveys—please!"
—MICKEY GROSSMAN, agent

"Actors dislike typing themselves. But everyone is a type. Julia Roberts is a leading-lady type. Brad Pitt is a leading-man type. Unless you're a lead—not in your opinion, but everyone else's that isn't related to you—you must type yourself. It helps you get jobs. Are you the funny next-door-neighbor type? Then be it and act it, even if you exaggerate it. They're always looking for funny next-door-neighbor types. Better an employed funny next-door-neighbor actor than a perpetually unemployed would-be leading man."
—DICK CLAIR, comedy writer (*The Carol Burnett Show*)

"I knew one didn't have to be handsome to work in movies and TV. And I'm better-looking than some of what I've seen. But I had to get used to the fact that my looks got me hired for a certain kind of role, and usually not a very large role. I do have these eyes, these teeth, and this high-dome forehead, but I do work more often than several actors I know." —VINCENT SCHIAVELLI (*Ghost*)

"Be prepared to have any and every aspect of your looks and weight dissected and criticized in front of your red face by the insensitive, not even beautiful or handsome people who do the hiring. It just goes with the territory. It's a meat market." —ROSIE O'DONNELL

"Had my nose been half an inch shorter, I might have been a devastating beauty. I'd have let my hair grow out, then. As it is, I don't mind being mistaken for a boy wearing lipstick." —BEATRICE LILLIE (*Thoroughly Modern Millie*)

"My nose was too 'cute' for drama—oh, and 'pert.' I was slotted into romantic comedies and such, while heavy dramas went to Davis and Stanwyck, etc. So be it. But then came the witch hunts, once Republicans took over the House and in effect targeted liberals, because you'd had [Franklin] Roosevelt in for four terms and then another Democrat, Harry Truman. Since I was pro-union, for peace and equal rights, etc., I was deprived of work—the studios, networks, sponsors, most of the media went along, all fooled or scared by McCarthy and company." —MARSHA HUNT (*Seven Sweethearts*)

"If you're asked, avoid politics unless you know who you're talking to. It's not as bad as when Congress set up its House Un-American Activities Committee and the White House wimped out on freedom, but it's still unwise. Note that John Wayne never suffered for his pro-war stance, but Jane Fonda, who opposed the war in Vietnam, nearly lost her career for it." —CHARLIE EARLE, publicist

"Don't lead with your religious or political convictions. If you're an actress, be aware that the power structure and media don't mind a man speaking up, but when women speak up, they often get put down. When you're starting out, be careful, though I don't say abandon your principles, as many have while trying to climb the showbiz ladder. In the past, several closeted men stars joined the Republicans, thinking the more antigay party would be better camouflage." —DANNY DEVITO

"As they say, everybody's a critic. In show business you get it from all sides. Better to censor yourself than have others do it for you . . . and learn to become open to your faults. When you watch and listen to yourself on the screen, learn to critique like a third person. Don't hate yourself, but don't love yourself. Change what needs changing. Even so, not everything needs changing, and not everything can be changed." —GERALDINE PAGE

"Get used to criticism. As if you have a choice! But the smartest thing to do is use it. Weigh what's been said to you—try and be objective. If what they've said has grounds to it, learn from it and incorporate it into your presentation. That's all criticism's good for— to instruct you." —DAVID J. STEWART, Broadway actor (*Antigone*)

"Casting people sometimes say the dumbest things. I would go audition for TV sitcoms during pilot season, and more than one so-called individual would

say to me, 'But you're Hispanic.' Yes. So? 'You are Hispanic.' I know that. Am I supposed to apologize, or is he asking me why I'm Hispanic? . . . Somehow, these people believed that being Hispanic, I wasn't supposed to try and be funny. I mean, go figure."
—FRANK MAYA, comedian

"Most stars are unique. But so are the memorable and more in-demand character actors. I know I'm unique. There's only one of me. Eventually I got more and more comfortable with that—the opposite of when you're in your teens—which is partly why I came out as bisexual. Why hide it? It's part of who I uniquely am—not that being bi is at all unique in Hollywood. But I put it all out there for the judges to see, and it worked. I'd get calls, I'd get offers. Not always my ideal offers, but offers. In this business, *an* offer is special." —ANDY DICK (MTV's *The Andy Dick Show*)

"Like nature, show business isn't fair. Say you have two blonde beauties. One opens her mouth and sounds like . . . Julie Christie. You think, ah, beauty, class, intelligence. The other opens her mouth— she's adenoidal and clearly from Brooklyn. You hire the Englishwoman. Obviously. However, anyone can work on their voice. Anyone can improve it. If they don't, they're lazy and not terribly ambitious." —IRVING RAPPER, English dialogue director turned movie director (*Now, Voyager*)

"Good-looking performers should not possess funny or offbeat voices. A rather deep voice on a beautiful actress is permissible. However, unusual voices otherwise limit acting opportunities. Funny, offbeat voices belong to comedy, where they're wonderful. Everything in its proper place." —HERMIONE GINGOLD, comedic actress (*A Little Night Music*)

"After I was hired, one of the casting persons said it had come down to me and an actor who looked more like what they wanted but didn't much connect with the other actor and hurried through his lines so much, some of the words were lost. Those things made him seem like he was standing waiting his turn to say something hopefully interesting. The c.d. said, 'He came off like a fast-talking mannequin.'" —JOCK MAHONEY, stuntman turned Tarzan, and Sally Field's stepfather

"Voice training is only partially for how an actor sounds. It has as much or more to do with pace and rhythm, modulation, contrast, emphasis, mood, implication . . . and more! It's why British and Aussie actors are so often hired to play American roles, but seldom American ones are hired to play British— or, in some cases, even regional American accents." —TESSA DEVERE, London vocal coach

"Some voices grate. How does yours affect people? A voice that sounds like a nagging wife will kill a non-comedic career. Make your voice suit your image. You wouldn't expect Garbo to sound like Minnie Mouse, would you?" —GUMMO MARX, agent, born a Marx Brother

"I studied with the great Michael Chekhov, so I know a few things about the voice and stillness. . . . The other week I saw a very good movie that was almost spoiled by terrible cinematography—if you want, look up the guy's name. The movie's story has a dark mood. So this guy lit it dark, and you could hardly see in half the scenes . . . worst-lit movie I've seen in years. The *performances* were where you'd get the dark mood—from their voices, their stillness, how they said what they said . . . and the actors were excellent! Luckily, you could always hear them, even if half the time you couldn't see them." —JACK PALANCE, on *Summer Wishes, Winter Dreams*

"It can almost break your heart. One actor recently did a fine audition. Then, instead of simply acknowledging us, saying goodbye and departing, his voice changed to a frustrated whine and he confessed he really so wanted to impress us and just knew he could do a better job, given another chance. But this was after six, seven minutes with us, and we had a line of other actors to see. I felt sorry for him, but one of the other two on my team said after this actor left, 'Was he trying for our sympathy? How pathetic.'" —OLIVIA HUNT, casting director

"When your audition's over, that's it. Over, finished. The easiest place on earth to overstay your welcome is at an audition. Make a smooth, clean exit. If they don't want you to go yet, they'll advise you, but nothing ticks them off like an actor who won't *go*." —SUSAN SARANDON

"Post-audition, make no comments on your perfor-mance. Not positive and certainly not negative. . . . These people most of the time don't know what they want, they're afraid to hire the 'wrong' actor 'cause it'll harm their next job. . . . Anything negative you say, and any klutzy gesture, any hanging on waiting for approval, those things are guaranteed detrimen-tal." —SAL MINEO (*Exodus*)

"The meeting or general meeting, whichever name they give it, is for personality and is overall a social thing. An audition is not a social thing. It's about per-formance—dozens of performances that we have to sit through, and the only way to leave a lasting positive memory is through your performance. Not through socializing and not through trying to network!" —FRAN BASCOM, casting director

"It can't be emphasized enough that unfortunately the actor who seems most to want or need the job rarely is the one to get it. Most producers, casting directors, and so forth are scared off by that sort of neediness or desperation." —TONY RICHARDSON, director (*Tom Jones*)

"I had the good fortune of wanting but not needing the job, and that's a huge thing—I was so scared about the five-year commitment that that took the edge off of the intimidation thing. . . . My fear of committing for five years helped me not be nervous in that audition." —HELEN HUNT, on landing the sitcom *Mad About You*

"After I stopped caring so much whether I got a particular role I was auditioning for, I began to get more of them. Of course I didn't truly stop caring, but I did get tired of having my hopes up so high that they'd typically come crashing down around me." —EVA LONGORIA (*Desperate Housewives*)

"It may be easier for men, but I think for an actress being comfortably clothed is significant toward doing well in an audition. I remember an audition I sat in on where one actress was almost spilling out of her top, and I wondered if she had to keep from bending or move in a certain way not to become frontally exposed. Unless of course that was her intention. She did not get the part. So there." —JULIE HARRIS

"I become comfortable by wearing something that is not restricting. My agent used to say, 'Wear three-inch heels because your legs look thinner.' I don't care at this point whether my legs look thinner. I will wear slacks now, cut very nicely with a waistband that is movable because my diaphragm expands [singing].

"Or something that won't show perspiration stains so that I have to keep my arms down. A hairdo that will not wilt the minute you walk out on stage, so that you don't have to worry about anything physical."
—KAREN MORROW, Broadway star who won an Emmy for *Cabaret Tonight* on PBS

"My type is buttoned-down. A suited-up executive. Not exactly comfortable, but I wouldn't get hired dressing collegiate or Hawaiian-tourist. . . . The other thing I soon learned was, being a straight man, I don't find anything funny. When I was with Lucy and Tallulah Bankhead and I got spray-painted, it was funny because I didn't think it was. Same on *Dick Van Dyke*. I get laughs from a situation. I do nothing. The star and/or the audience does it."
—RICHARD DEACON (*The Dick Van Dyke Show*)

"Early on, I'd get blue auditioning, because I was so different I figured I didn't have a chance. Then I got on *Welcome Back, Kotter*, it became a hit show, and while it ran it was heaven. I was in supporting, but it was national, and the fans loved me. After, what got me back to being blue was I'd go to auditions and they'd call me 'Horshack,' not my own name, plus the usual curse of being too associated with a famous role. Hundreds of lucky TV actors have been through that.

"So it all but forces you to go back to the stage, which is where most East Coast actors began anyway. Television can so spoil you." —RON PALILLO

"It's inside of most actors to want to expand and show their range; but I tell ya, once you've gone top-rated in a long-running TV role, that sticks to you like a mask. The public prefers it and the casting directors insist on it . . . I wanted to play some interesting villains. I played one, really, in a fine movie, *A Face in the Crowd*. But that was before I became a sheriff [Sheriff Andy Taylor]. I didn't get the same kind of chance again." —ANDY GRIFFITH

"Most recognizable actors today are recognized from television, not from the movies. But that lovely weekly paycheck will only last so many years, so save your pennies, my darlings. Also, keep your other options open—film, stage, commercials, a possible talk show, a book, a nightclub act. Casting people are amazingly quick to stick you into a pigeonhole, and unless you really are versatile and determined, in that pigeonhole you shall remain." —NATALIE SCHAFER (*Gilligan's Island*)

"Before you go on an audition, try and know—in fact, try and do this before you sign with an agent—try to find out what side he's on. What I mean is: I always told my agents, I want the career, not the money. Whether they listened or not is another thing, but I wanted them to send me out for opportunities, for the long run. Not for any old paying gig. Some gigs can harm your reputation . . . the word about desperation gets around.

"Don't take something just because it pays. Is it right for you? Does it enhance and help build you? And is your agent helping build you?" —DAVID GROH (*Rhoda*)

"Strange as it may seem, there are some agents who are uncomfortable handling a big star. They're more comfortable with, at most, a midsized star. The responsibilities and pressure, and the spotlight, of handling a major star make them nervous, insecure. . . . Such agents aren't usually at the biggest agencies, but there are a few agents at the big agencies who prefer being better known in the industry than their own clients. Jealousy of a client does happen. . . ." —MICKEY GROSSMAN, agent

"But some agents just want their ten percent—of whatever, and whether or not it helps their clients over the long haul. I wanted career, because once you attain that, then the money comes anyway." —BILLY CRYSTAL

"Like many newcomers, I didn't know that when you wanted feedback about your audition, you don't ask the casting director, you go back and ask your agent. A good agent will usually find out how

it went. If an agent gets upset with you for asking, it's time to start hunting for a new agent. A piece of advice: don't get angry at your agent until you've lined up a new one, and even then. People do go back to their old agents, for one reason or another."
—KERWIN MATHEWS (*The 7th Voyage of Sinbad*)

"I told an acting coach [that] auditioning made me kind of angry. I auditioned for him, and he said he could see that. So the choice was: to audition or not? If I did want to do it, I had to give up the anger and resentment of doing it. Once I made that choice, it was easy for me to eliminate it, and auditioning became fun. I came to the point where I really liked to audition." —DARRYL HICKMAN (*The Many Loves of Dobie Gillis*)

"What turns me off in auditions isn't what they expect me to do; after all, I chose this. It's the occasional indifference or the sometimes appalling inattentiveness on the auditors' part. Ideally, they're welcoming and attentive. Realistically, not always . . . and to rise above that takes true willpower. You need to focus strongly and hopefully, and to assume somebody there is paying attention." —PERRY LOPEZ (*The Two Jakes*)

"I've been to auditions where the person in charge was a slob—the one who sets the tone for the rest of his team. . . . What you hopefully discover from your agent or by word of mouth if the casting head is rude is that he's rude to everyone. That's better, 'cause then you don't have to get upset or downhearted, because it's not personal." —ROBERT WEBBER (*10*)

"If you suffer from depression, show business is not the place to show it . . . I used to advise my pupils, '*Toujours gai*, kids, *toujours gai*,' till *gai*, which means *gay*, changed its meaning." —NINA FOCH, actor-coach

"Marlon gets a kick out of extremely outgoing personalities. He's very shy at heart, but knows how to cover it. What I've seen is extravagantly friendly, loud personalities who'll go in and charm or delight the audition people but infrequently go beyond them, because audition people are afraid to hire them. They fear that those brassy, how-ya-doin' types will disrupt a set." —PHIL RHODES, Brando's lifelong makeup artist

"Don't schmooze. Almost invariably, schmoozers get made fun of the minute they leave the room. It's generally considered unprofessional, and by some feel the actor's trying to make up with personality and glad-handing for a lack of acting talent." —DANIEL MELNICK, producer (*All That Jazz*)

"I have seen more people come in and engage us in conversation and be charming and witty and funny and give us a great expectation as to, 'Oh, my goodness, this is so terrific I can't wait till they read.' And

then they stink in the reading and we're so disappointed by it because of the table that was set by them.

"All you have to do as an auditioning person is come
in, make eye contact with the people in the room, say
hello, and do the scene." —MICHAEL LEMBECK,
TV director

"The phenomena of extra population, stronger bugs,
and germ-consciousness have cut down, in many cases
completely, on shaking hands at auditions. If a hand
is offered, shake it. But don't initiate it. A nod of the
head, a smile . . . that South Asian greeting with the
palms of your hands pressed together is also appropriate—and distinctive." —Sir MICHAEL GAMBON,
Dumbledore in the *Harry Potter* films

"The only person you're allowed to touch or more
or less handle at an audition is the actor you audition
with, if there's another actor. Regardless of written
directions, don't get too rough. You only have to indicate violence or passion . . . don't set yourself up
for a possible lawsuit with witnesses present by hitting
and injuring another guy or ripping the blouse of an
actress—which has actually happened. As professionals, actors should know their limits." —FREDDIE
FIELDS, agent

"You can't know how you've affected those watching you audition. So you need to be neutral and calm
about it all. If you felt an audition went badly, yours

might be the minority opinion. But once you've said, 'Oh, shit,' or, 'That was lousy,' you start to convince the rest of them." —COLIN FIRTH (*Apartment Zero*)

"If one feels an audition hasn't gone well, try not to let on in front of the judges. An expression of composure, come fair, come foul." —Dame MAGGIE SMITH, two-time Oscar winner

"Casting people have memories like elephants. Remember that, in anything you say or do outside of the lines you're reading and bringing to life. Don't give 'em cause to remember you in any negative way." —PAUL WINFIELD (*Sounder*)

"Mirroring the times, there are more homeless characters . . . I recall a series of auditions for men playing homeless where about half of all the actors submitted not only looked awful, they smelled awful. Well! Acting is not reality, it is a representation of reality, and out of hand I dismissed all the stinking actors.

"It may be they'd all heard that Nick Nolte literally stank on the set of *Down and Out in Beverly Hills*. Well, he was foolish, but he was a star. These men were foolish and not stars." —PAT BROOKS, casting director

"Casting directors can be pretty good actors themselves. I remember hearing, years later, that a particular c.d. used to 'cringe' in my presence because he thought I was coming on too strong and chummy. Not sexual, mind you, just 'overly friendly,' to use his very words." —PATSY KELLY, golden-era character star

"My father once said, 'Don't you ever apologize for who you are. Ever!' I never ever walked in [to a casting director's office] saying, 'Oh, God, you're so great for seeing me.'" —RICHARD DREYFUSS

"Casting directors are, or have, the keys to the kingdom. So there is a tendency for aspiring actors to try too hard with them or try and be endearing, especially in opposite-sex situations. We casting directors don't want to play mama or papa or big brother or confidant, we only want to discover and promote talent. . . . If in time we do become friendly with actors, then it's appropriate; an acquaintance should not act like an old friend." —LYNN STALMASTER

"All actors are insecure. That's very appealing. In the beginning I was amazed what actors worried about. Here they were, great-looking—I mean *great*—and how many of them told me they believed their names were too common or their names were too weird. No problem! They had star quality. They were wearing it, permanently, at least for a decade or two.

"Besides, I simply changed names like Merle Johnson and Arthur Gelien and Roy Fitzgerald to

Troy Donahue, Tab Hunter, and Rock Hudson."
—HENRY WILLSON, agent

"Nervousness is always apparent, and nervousness is a touching and good quality. Everybody understands what nervousness is, and nobody has ever held it against an actor." —STEPHEN SONDHEIM

"A casting associate admitted that a few times *she* got nervous when a spectacularly beautiful actress walked into the room . . . and that if the actress wasn't humble or modest, she felt disinclined to choose her for a part. I asked, 'What if she was talented?' My friend said, 'No one believes a beautiful woman is talented.' I'd say the lesson is: if you're stunning, be nice, to make up for it."
—JAMES BRIDGES, director (*Perfect*)

"I didn't want an acting career that was defined and limited by my looks, and later I rebelled against that sort of casting very strongly. But going in, I wasn't in the best position, coming as I did from the field of modeling." —JESSICA LANGE, eventual two-time Oscar winner

"People who knew me knew how beautiful I was. But I had to have *all* of [their approval] to see how beautiful I was. I had to show to them all that I looked like a movie star. So I started my campaign to go to all of the nightclubs. I pretended to see, so I could be seen!"
—MARIA MONTEZ (*Cobra Woman*), who made a

point of being widely seen by industry honchos and frequently photographed and publicized

"Star quality used to be equated with breeding and dressing well. I still believe that good clothes have a lot to do with good manners. . . . Young actresses would scrimp and save to spend on clothes that would help distinguish them in public. Standing out, *above* the crowd, was considered essential to working your way up the ladder in pictures." —JOAN CRAWFORD, who had a special outfit for answering fan mail

"Professional quality comes through in not acting juvenile or shocked by industry requirements. Such as, in real life two men don't usually stand very close while talking . . . not in English-speaking countries. The camera often requires it. So you'll be intimately close—preferably minus smirks, jokes, or hesitation—but you'll comfortably and convincingly read your non-intimate lines. . . . Even if you're new to this business, try to behave maturely." —MICHAEL SARRAZIN (*They Shoot Horses, Don't They?*)

"I hear that more auditions are filmed now, not just for commercials . . . so actors need to be more camera-conscious. You need to ask, if you're to be filmed, how much appears in the shot. So that, say, if your hands are doing or holding something, you'll raise them in a natural-looking way and they'll end up in the shot." —ELI WALLACH (*Baby Doll*)

"Life and acting overlap; they aren't the same. In people-eating-at-a-table scenes, there's always that empty space in front of the camera so viewers can see everyone, or at least part of everyone's face. Actors have to learn to make any situation look natural . . . they have to appear comfortable and natural and even indifferent, like people do in real life." —SHARON GLESS (*Cagney and Lacey*)

"I never was great at cold readings, so I'd sort of mask my lack of confidence with indifference. I don't know, maybe it came across as arrogance sometimes. Main thing is, in acting more than in most endeavors, you try to conceal your liabilities. Actually, though, there isn't any business where you don't act." —ROBERT DE NIRO

"I chatted with the princess, who I remembered in movies when she was Grace Kelly, the star from Philadelphia. When I asked if she missed acting, she smiled and said, 'What do you think I'm doing now?'" —PENNY MARSHALL, actor-director (*A League of Their Own*)

"If you dress like a tart, you'll be treated like one. If you dress like a princess, you'll be admired or desired or pitied, depending. Dress with dignity. Walk with dignity. . . . The longer an actress stays in the business, the more they try to strip away her dignity. That's why so many actresses, compared to actors, leave the business later—or sometimes sooner." —BRENDA FRICKER, Oscar winner for *My Left Foot*

"In this business, a little dignity is required, minimum. A smile may help; too many may undo you." —NICOLE KIDMAN

"Familiarity breeds attempt." —JAYNE MANSFIELD

"An actress doesn't want to seem easy. There *is* such a thing as a casting couch—I think there always will be. But unless you have the acting chops of Meryl Streep or the balls of someone like Bette Davis, you have to kind of ingratiate yourself to the men in power. And so, very often, that gets mistaken for being easy." —ANITA MORRIS (*Nine* on Broadway)

"If you have self-esteem you'll be treated accordingly. If not, you won't. The actor sets the tone of the relationship. That's what did poor Marilyn Monroe in. Despite her looks, it came across that she was needy and unsure." —Sir BEN KINGSLEY

"A valuable tip passed on to me by a temporarily traumatized actor is that you shouldn't be overly deferential when you reach the level of interviewing with a director or producer, no matter how famous. They may read that as a potential doormat for them to walk over if they hire you. A good beginning makes for a good ending." —AMY ADAMS (*Doubt*)

"Acting teachers advise you to just be yourself during an interview with an agent or casting director. Not necessarily! If your self isn't replete with self-esteem and other starry qualities, *act* it. Pretend to be that self. Isn't that what acting is? *Be* that character who goes into the interview or audition. If you do it often enough, it becomes second nature." —DAVID HYDE PIERCE (*Frasier*)

"Everybody wants to be Cary Grant. I want to be Cary Grant." —CARY GRANT, the officially heterosexual icon born Archibald Leach

"Don't resent auditioning. It's necessary. Even stars audition; you just don't hear much about it. If you keep resenting auditions, it will show, believe me. Unless you're a superb actor. Actually, I think it was Nietzsche who said, 'If thou gaze too long into the abyss, the abyss will gaze into thee.' Ponder *that*." —WOODY ALLEN

"I wasn't down on casting directors, like so many actors are. Most casting directors are failed actors. What I resented was how 'little people' have to audition, while stars just read a script, say yes, then a movie gets made. Or so I thought. Everything's much more complicated than that." —RUE MCCLANAHAN (*The Golden Girls*)

"I got in the Screen Actors Guild back in the early

'50s. Walter Pidgeon was the president then . . . I remember calling my parents and saying I'm in the same union with Walter Pidgeon, Cagney and Cooper and Barbara Stanwyck and Bette Davis—all these fabulous people that I grew up [watching]. And I thought I was hot stuff, until I started knocking on doors and getting the turndowns.

"So I appreciate everything that all actors in the Guild have had to go through at some time in their life." —CLINT EASTWOOD

"Ours is not a union, it's a guild. We keep our heads high because it's such an iffy, sometimes dispiriting business. Unemployment is the norm. . . . We fought long and hard to gain the right to have decent pay and safe working conditions. Did you know the Academy—that group with the awards—was originally formed by the movie studios to prevent unionization? It's all too true." —LAUREN BACALL

"You can inform your non-actor friends that 'casting director' is only an informal term. We do not direct, and officially, in screen credits, only three professions may use the word 'director': the director, the director of photography, and the art director. Our screen credit simply reads 'casting' or 'casting by.'"
—STANLEY SOBLE, Casting Society of America

"I used to begrudge the power of casting directors. Then I soured on how rare auditions are. Finally I wised up and saw auditions for what they were: a precious opportunity to perform before professionals, improve my craft, and impress the c.d. so she'll pass me on to the higher power who can hire me. Now I welcome each and every audition." —SIENNA MILLER

"It seems to me that in this business of acting it's not about doing good work so much as it is about being given the chance to do good work." —HUGH LAURIE (*House*)

"Above all else, no matter how badly you need work, no matter how hungry you are, how exhausted you've become from playing duck-the-landlord, never, ever show desperation." —MICHAEL J. FOX

"What happens is, if they think you're desperate for the role, they won't give it to you. They don't want a desperate actor on set. If you seem unconcerned whether you get the role or not, your chances of getting it are vastly improved. It's sort of like banking—you only get the loan if you don't really need it." —MICHAEL MCDONALD (*MADtv*), who worked as a bank teller

"If I went in for a role and I heard back that I wasn't right for it, I would always say, 'They made a huge mistake.' Rarely would it hurt my feelings. Nothing would set me back." —TERI GARR (*Tootsie*)

"You have to think of yourself as that toy that looks like a clown, with sand on the bottom, then when you punch it, it comes right back up. . . . You cannot allow yourself to be defined by rejection." —HENRY WINKLER (*Happy Days*)

"My real name is Ophelia, so you'd think I was born to do the classics. So did I. But when I stepped onto a real live stage, I felt happy and kind of giddy. I smiled and giggled, and the audience laughed, and I enjoyed their laughter. So my career in comedy took off in spite of my intentions and inclinations." —MINNIE PEARL, country comic

"Did you know I started out as a standup comic? People don't believe me when I tell them. . . . That's how I saw myself, in comedy, and I didn't know I would do this with my life. I didn't know what the hell I was going to do." —AL PACINO

"The guys auditioning you aren't there to judge you or put you down. They're there trying to find the best actor—in their opinion or opinions—for the role. The sooner they find him, the sooner they can go home. They want you to be good!" —BOB DENVER (*Gilligan's Island*)

"Some talents aren't good at auditions, are lousy at cold readings. If I sense that, I try to give them more time. They may be fine after they've memorized their lines

and assumed the character. Problem is, there's so little time. I may have to see or read six actors in 30 minutes. Something about an actor has to stand out for me to take the extra time to probe and guide that actor."
—JOY TODD, casting director

"Like many casting people, I was an actor, so I have empathy for what actors go through. . . . Various actors close up during auditions—a no-no. Classes for cold-reading and auditions and auditioning for commercials are a must for actors who won't open up. . . . Even in general interviews, some actors' personalities don't come through—sometimes they don't want it to come through." —PAT MCWILLIAMS

"The bow never means anything for me. I'm always embarrassed to take a bow. I would rather not take a bow. My coming out and taking a bow, a curtain call—I'm Ron, and I don't want to be there as Ron."
—RON RIFKIN

"Actors can't know the reasons they're not picked. . . . Hair color, height, too this, too that. One fine actress was vetoed by a producer because she resembled his ex-wife, whom he hated. You may read wonderfully, but we're looking for someone more, uh, less literate. Or you keep substituting words. It could be anything. It's not a personal rejection. Don't sweat it. Move on." —ED LIMATO, agent

"I used to audition a lot for commercials in New York. One morning I auditioned for two voiceovers. The second one, I felt I did a third-rate job. But they hired me. Eventually the producer admitted I'd done a terrible job auditioning. I asked why on earth they'd hired me. He said they'd been looking for someone who read badly, and I was the best at it." —LOUIS ZORICH (*Dirty Rotten Scoundrels*)

"At an audition, the casting director and the director, if he's there, may ask you to reread or do something slightly or completely differently. Even if it sounds odd, do it. They're testing to see how well you take direction. . . . Often, a director asks for a different mood or emotion and the actor eagerly says okay, then proceeds to read it exactly the same way as before! Well, that's the kiss of death.

"You should listen closely to directions, then follow them." —VICTORIA PRINCIPAL, former agent and actor

"Cardinal rule for an auditioning actor: do not touch or unduly frighten the casting person. Even if you're auditioning for Jack the Ripper. Hands off. Don't invade their space. And do not rearrange things on their desk—which I've seen happen. Those people have long memories, and you may never get to audition for them again." —RON SILVER (*Reversal of Fortune*)

"If you think you turned in a great audition, you

probably but not necessarily did. If you did, and you didn't get the job, we'll remember you and may call you in later for something we think you're right for. Auditions that don't result in jobs still result in future opportunities for jobs." —MARY V. BUCK, casting director

"First, don't show up in costume. That's for amateurs. Wear clothes that suggest the character. You don't wish to seem gimmicky or overeager. And come as yourself, not the character. I've had actors auditioning for psychos come bursting into the office full of threat and menace. That makes me wonder if it's the actor's real personality. Once you start reading the part, you can go full-throttle. We like to know that we're dealing with rational, responsible individuals." —RISA BRAMON GARCIA, casting director

"When I first auditioned, I was told that I could hardly read, let alone act. I'd wrongly assumed that acting was no more difficult than being a porter or a janitor, a dishwasher or a garage attendant, all of which I'd tried for. So I set about educating and improving myself as best I could. I worked nights, and I'd study the newspaper religiously during my meal breaks at the restaurant. Fortunately, an old Jewish waiter who also worked there noticed me and what I was trying to do. He took pity on me and became my tutor, my guardian angel . . . he helped me to learn to read." —SIDNEY POITIER

"One reason it took time to become successful is my face. Never a beauty. And though I was a feminist and took my mother's birth name and became famous for having limo companies hire female chauffeurs once I got top billing, I often came across to casting agents as weak or funny and weak.

"All I can say is, some of us are meant to be discovered at a later age. But you don't give up— or you won't get discovered at a later age! . . . The key thing is enjoying what you're doing while you're hoping to be discovered." —JEAN STAPLETON (*All in the Family*)

"If you achieve stardom, you'll be surprised, at several points, how little it can come to mean. There are more perks, true. There are also far more headaches, and a far greater need to beware of people inside and outside the business. Whereas on the stage, when you're doing really fine work, it can lift you out of yourself, to a spiritual high so satisfying and proud-making that you can't wait to re-create it—and you know you will." —CLAUDETTE COLBERT, Oscar winner for *It Happened One Night*

"An audition is a performance, and once you're acclimated to auditions, it is possible to soar in them, depending on the material, the circumstances, and the serendipity of the moment. It's happened to me a handful of times—sort of an ecstasy . . . later I looked the word up, and it [*extasis*] means, from

the classical Greek, to stand outside of oneself. Which is what lucky actors sometimes experience."
—LYNN REDGRAVE

"Just as you'll have all sorts of casting directors and experiences, there's all sorts of directors. The best way to learn acting—and for that matter, auditioning effectively—is working with a variety of directors. That'll make you flexible and capable in any number of situations."
—BRAD RENFRO (*The Client*)

"Sometimes the smartest opening move an aspiring actor can make is learning to act so that his contempt for auditions or his fear of them doesn't show. . . . Some of it's common sense, of course, like not walking in with a chip on your shoulder or acting like we're wasting *your* time, not saying 'shit' and 'fuck' for the sake or habit of it, etc. But do learn to act like you're pleased to attend the audition. Not overjoyed, but pleased and willing."
—BILL GRADY, MGM casting director

"What's with all this foul language from actors now? Even actresses talk out of the gutter. Trying to prove . . . what? How common or uneducated they are? That's all their four-letter words prove to me. I'd say a little class is not only desirable, it's a requirement."
—SAM COHN, agent

"When you come into my office, you're in my professional home. You're a guest. Do not swear, don't chew

gum, don't act like we're at a pool hall. If you want to be respected, not to mention hired, show some respect."
—JOHN HOUSEMAN, producer and co-creator of the Juilliard School

"One of my biggest booboos was recommending a talented comedian and good actor with bad manners. I was later apprised that on the job he looked down on several crew members and made jokes at their expense. Never look down on the crew. They're very talented at what they do. They can also help you. . . ."
—MARY V. BUCK, casting director

"As with most of Western civilization, it goes back to ancient Greece, where they had a music-and-dancing festival called a *komos*. Its leading entertainer was the *komoidos*, from which evolved the comedian."
—HARVEY LEMBECK, actor and creator of The Comedy Workshop

"Having a sense of when to speak and when not to speak is important for any actor, in auditions and in the work. But it's more important for a comedian. Too much talk can kill the comedy." —TINA FEY

"I've become famous for my pauses. Fortunately, they went over even in radio. That shows that pauses can be funny and meaningful." —JACK BENNY

"Timing is the top requirement of comedy. A good

joke without good timing is nothing, whereas a bad joke with good timing can work out so-so. . . . Timing can be improved. It cannot be taught." —CHEVY CHASE (*Saturday Night Live*)

"My laugh became one of my biggest trademarks. When I first laughed on a stage, I bet I did it because no one else was laughing—trying to prime the pump, you know. And it helped. But then some people would say, 'She laughs too much,' or, 'She has such a crazy laugh.' But I kept it, and years later I sometimes got hired for my famous laugh—just to do the laugh, nothing else! So stick with your instincts." —PHYLLIS DILLER

"Laughter spreads. . . . If you are sitting in a restaurant, 50 people may recognize you, but if nobody asks for that first autograph, you can eat your whole meal and no one will ask you. But if one person asks, guaranteed within the next half hour everybody there will ask. Same thing with laughter. If somebody starts laughing out loud, it begins to get around." —WOODY ALLEN

"Even before you're hired to act, knowing people, reading people, reacting and adapting to people is invaluable. As in an audition room. By the time you do your first audition, you should have been observing and studying people for years. That's what it takes to act and to succeed as an actor. It develops

you and your interactions with others. Crucial stuff!"
—BEATRICE ARTHUR

"University did help me, because comedy requires a lot of discipline. Jokes are not easy to write and comedic thinking, if it's good, is very disciplined. There has got to be a very strong logic and some real point to it. But the most important thing was that I finished college. That set up a pattern of finishing things and seeing it through. In doing stand-up, you encounter resistance and it is good to have that pattern in your life to keep going." —JERRY SEINFELD

"Interesting, the differences in public reactions. Two women see a handsome movie star and they'll whisper to each other about him and they're thrilled and embarrassed and usually keep their distance. When they see a famous comedian, their faces open up and they'll rush up to you and say whatever's on their mind, pro or con." —JERRY LEWIS

"A comic is still the court jester. You're judged more harshly. A dramatic actor is given more respect, more leeway. But if you're a comedian, people feel free to tell each other—or even you—'He's not so funny. I don't think he's funny.' Then sometimes they'll name someone who they do think is funny." —MICHAEL MCDONALD (*MADtv*)

"I remember hearing a comedian tell how a friend's husband had just died, and the woman was so sad. But after half an hour, the comedian got a belly laugh out of her. To me, that's like medicine. It's as good as what a doctor does and better than what most shrinks do. Making laughter and bringing out wide smiles is something to be real proud of." —CHRIS ROCK

"Some young people are drawn to comedy because they think they don't have to learn lines. Other people's lines, anyway. Or it looks easier than drama—*hah!* If you want to go into comedy, whether as a standup or as a funny actor, ask yourself, are you a funny person and do you have a comic outlook on life? If you're not sure, then you're not and you don't. These things one knows by age 12.

"Also, do you enjoy being in front of a crowd? Do you know when to pause for effect, when to let the laughter continue and when to cut it short? Are you very resistant to criticism? Do you believe you're special and have something unique to say and in a unique way? Do you? *Well?*" —DON RICKLES

"So often, even when I was starting out and audition-ing, I would do routines that were meant to sound like adlibbing. But I'd worked on them and polished them so they sounded unrehearsed. . . . Some people would pass on hiring me, saying I adlibbed too much. Others thought it all came too easily to me. What most people in or out of the business don't always re-

alize is that when it looks easy, they're looking at art."
—ROBIN WILLIAMS

"One good tip for actors who perform live, including on Broadway, is to not compare audiences. 'Last night's audience was better than tonight's.' 'Cause when you do that, you're really rating yourself, and subconsciously blaming yourself. You can't control audiences, and you shouldn't commence a deterioration of your own ego." —GILDA RADNER (*Saturday Night Live*)

"Most [comedians], they get a bad audience, they panic, they get jangled and they get ugly, they get hostile. They get hecklers and they talk back and they get evil and every time they do that they're weakening and being unprofessional. And every time you're unprofessional, every time you're undisciplined, it's easier to do it again. First thing you know, they've lost everything." —PHYLLIS DILLER

"There's a male comedian, a minority comedian, and my guess is he's chosen to let bigotry infect him. He's not strong enough to shrug it off, to proceed regardless. Maybe he imagines bigotry where it doesn't exist. Bill Cosby was as big as anyone, and he had the right attitude. But now and then this guy behaves self-destructively and unprofessionally. His career's in the balance, and if he thinks talent excuses his behavior . . . he'll find out."—SID CAESAR

"What one finds funny, another doesn't. What one finds innocent, the other sees something lewd in it. Like with censors, who typically have dirty minds. It recalls the story of a long-ago censor who banned a song titled 'She Sits Among the Cabbages and Peas.' The composer changed the title, and the censor said it was all right: 'She Sits Among the Lettuces and Leeks.'" —FRANKIE HOWERD, British comedian

"Why there are so many fewer female comedians is because it's so tough and punishing when you become a standup comic. Audiences challenge a comedienne; they dare her to be funny—funnier than a guy. . . . If women had to go in the army like men used to, they'd be tougher. It's not a pretty business, and it's mean. Men usually expect that, but with women, well, it depends. The sensitive ones won't last, and this might be a stereotype, but it's true: really tough women stick it out longer and can find success, which is a big reason so many successful female comics are lesbians." —WANDA SYKES

"A comic actor, even more than other actors, is a leader. You lead your listeners and viewers to where you want to take them. They're there to be led. They want to be led. So you have to be very sure of yourself. You have to be confident, and if one thing doesn't work, you try another. You can't be a one-trick pony.

That's why beautiful women don't usually make good comedians. It's all they have. A sex symbol has sex and practically nothing else." —JAY LENO

"Really good-looking people haven't had to work on their personalities. They can get by on their looks— till they lose them. I mean, name a really attractive comedian, male or female. . . . Almost by definition, beauty queens are shallow." —DANNY THOMAS (*Make Room for Daddy*)

"Growing up without a father, I became more blunt. Most girls sidle up to their fathers, they flirt, they play a game to get what they want. I just asked for what I wanted." —BARBRA STREISAND

"There are exceptions to this, but most of the funny men I know, the comics, they got along swell with their mothers. They saw the laughter. The men who hated their mothers, they either became dramatic actors or conservative politicians or something else. Mothers can help their boys see the lighter side of life." —DON KNOTTS (*The Andy Griffith Show*)

"It's sad when you think about it, how some men think they're born comedians and they aren't even funny. The laughter that follows their jokes is mostly their own or else that of people trying to curry favor. Jack Warner was like that—to the very end, he was convinced he was funny and the life of the party." —BETTE DAVIS, known in her heyday as the "fifth Warner Brother"

"A common mistake made by comedically oriented actors attempting drama is talking too loud. They think loud equals intense. No. Loud equals noisy. Intensity equals energy . . . the way an actor manifests energy is via intensity. A quiet, important talk between two characters needs intense energy. It doesn't need volume, which would diminish it." —JOY TODD, casting director

"Before an audition, rehearse your business—of course props and auditions don't usually mix. But rehearse your business and ideas and movements, without setting them down in stone. It should help you feel more comfortable, during. Of course during the audition, go with the flow, and spontaneously change anything except the dialogue, as the inspiration strikes you." —ROSCOE LEE BROWNE (*The Mambo Kings*)

"Be fluid and adaptable. When you rehearse at home, try different ways of saying the lines, of moving with them, of reacting to the other actor's lines. The more variations you have, the more you can offer at the audition when you're asked to do it another way." —JENNIFER BEALS (*Flashdance*)

"The reason rehearsing on your own, pre-audition, is not a waste of time is that it is nowadays often a necessity. It's the most rehearsal you'll get! Commercials, I don't do commercials, but in movies there's minimal rehearsal, if any. In television, with the backbreaking deadlines, none! So we want to see, and for TV we need to see, thought-out, polished performances." —GERMAINE BOUCHARD, casting director

"If the c.d. doesn't tell you, your agent or manager will: that a movie audition cuts you some slack, because if they like you, they can work with you and improve what you've shown them. If it's a TV audition, they want to see the finished product. Man, your TV audition has to be as good as what you would do in front of the TV cameras." —GEORGE LOPEZ (*The George Lopez Show*)

"You do the audition. You get called back. You get hired! You celebrate! Then you start to sweat. Because—have you ever thought about this?—when you're shooting that film that's going to take seven or eight weeks, you have to be, or ought to be, as good playing that character on the first day as on the last day. . . . My God!" —ANNE HECHE (*Volcano*)

"It takes time and creative exploration to get inside a character. That's why frightened actors and lazy actors, also some star actors, may forego the character and lapse into being their own selves. It's a habit to avoid, unless one is an ongoingly popular star who doesn't read reviews." —Sir IAN MCKELLEN, Magneto in the *X-Men* trilogy

"It's not about becoming someone else; it's about *you* interpreting someone else . . . a magic meld." —TONI COLLETTE (*Muriel's Wedding*)

"Auditioning's not easy, but it does come down to performing. In a way, it should be less nerve-wracking than performing in front of a hundred people. True, this one or these few people can lead to the next step in your getting hired, but . . . well, isn't that all the more reason to want to be a good auditioner?" —BERNIE BRILLSTEIN, manager

"There's no way around auditions, kids. There's just one way: to get better at them. The more you do them, the better you'll get. Once you've been hired, you'll feel differently about auditions, I promise you." —CLORIS LEACHMAN, Oscar winner

"Quit whining and start refining. Keep getting better and better, not better and bitter. The bitter will show, unless you're a consistently fabulous actor. The better shows too. Fortunately." —MEL BROOKS

"It doesn't hurt to feel glad or even grateful that you did the audition. Many others wanted to. But *you* got to. Your foot's in the door, anything can happen. . . .

Like they say, you can't win if you're not at the table."
—BROOKE SHIELDS

"In an audition, as in a performance, an actor should remember that *he* shouldn't be affected by *them. They* should be affected by *you.*" —JOE WIZAN, agent turned head of 20th Century-Fox

3

CONNECTING

"For most actors, your first and last connection is to the camera. It is your #1 audience and your audience of one. Share with the camera, make love to the camera, never fear the camera." —JACK LEMMON

"If you can't see the camera, it can't see you. Always keep that in the middle of your mind." —MICHEL ST. DENIS, co-creator of the Juilliard School

"If two people are positioned talking in front of a camera, both need to be sure that most of their face or at least their profile is visible to the camera. . . . If the person nearer the camera turns naturally to the one behind her, most of her face won't be seen. You must 'cheat' for the camera so that the audience sees what it's supposed to see." —RUSSELL METTY, cinematographer (*Spartacus*)

"As I stood by the camera waiting for my cue, the cameraman said, 'Will the tall girl move a few inches to the right?' Bette Davis must have seen my involuntary wince because she put up her hand and said, 'Her name is Marian Seldes.' Afterward she told me, 'At Warners, when I was a star, I introduced everyone on the set.'" —MARIAN SELDES, Broadway star (*Equus*)

"The big disconnect for an actor is when he adds or subtracts words or lines. Don't do that! You might add ideas or business. You disconnect from professionalism when you start rearranging the script, which you have been hired to interpret, not revise." —MIKE NICHOLS, director (*The Graduate*)

"Acting is connecting . . . and connections. Connecting with your feelings and with fellow actors. Necessarily, making the connections to get the role, which requires connecting with *those* people, face to face, eyes to eyes." —JASON ALEXANDER (*Seinfeld*)

"The better and more comfortably you can connect with people on all levels, the better your future in acting." —ALLAN CARR, producer (*Grease*)

"Acting is about people. Other people. Otherwise, you're not acting, you're doing monologues." —DANIEL DAY-LEWIS

"More accurately, acting could be labeled 'interacting,' because that's what happens. You can act in a soliloquy, but you can only interact with or react off another person." —Sir CAROL REED, director

"I had a, let's say, 'Mediterranean' neighbor . . . a seamstress who loved expressing herself. She'd unloosen her emotions and vent her voice at the drop of a feathered hat. She often said she could have been a great actress if only acting paid steadily. I secretly disagreed, and why? Her emotions rotated around herself. She seldom related to other people, except as her customers or her audience." —TOM CONTI, British actor (*Shirley Valentine*)

"There has to be some sensitivity toward other people. A total narcissist is probably incapable of simulating, let alone feeling, the emotions that acting requires." —REESE WITHERSPOON

"How do you react to other people as a private person? How do you react to others on a stage or before a camera? *Do* you react to them? Or are you just waiting for your turn to speak? And, just as crucially, how do you react to potential employers?" —LOU JACOBI (*Irma la Douce*)

"Not just drama, but comedy too, they all revolve around conflict. To have—that is, to be able to

illustrate—conflict, more than one person is essential."
—Dame MAGGIE SMITH

"It must be wonderful to create the finished product all by yourself. Like a writer with a book. But actors can make much more money than most writers, plus they get recognized on the street." —DREW BARRYMORE at 15

"It's harder when you get recognized in a restaurant while you're eating or in a bathroom . . . and you can't be nasty to the fans. Word gets around quickly when stars do that." —DREW BARRYMORE at 27

"A woman rushed up to me the other day, all aglow. She said, 'I recognized you right away! You know how?' 'How?' I asked. She was so enthused, dying to explain. 'Your *face!*'" —CAROL BURNETT

"There's fame and there's fortune. I think most of us who have had both, if we had to choose only one, would choose fortune." —ALAN ALDA

"One can be a very successful writer and not meet one's readers, or, as some insist on calling themselves, 'fans.' But even mildly successful actors and actresses have encounters with fans. It's unavoidable." —COLIN FIRTH (*A Single Man*)

"If you choose acting, you're choosing people. Lots and lots of people. Remember that, so maybe you won't complain so much later. After all, it's your choice. A choice many people, including your parents, will try and talk you out of. You make your bed, you have to lie in it." —PAUL SORVINO, father of Mira

"Acting is a people business. If you're a painter, sculptor, writer, or poet, you can work alone. Not an actor. Even the one-person stage show—which usually stars somebody famous, in the second half of their career—requires a writer, a director, and an entire crew.

"So you must develop your social skills as well as your proverbial instrument. It's people who hire you, people that you work with, and an army of people you have to get along with, or at least pretend to." —MARTIN FREEMAN, Bilbo Baggins in *The Hobbit*

"Network, network, network. You never know who knows somebody. You never know who will become somebody." —FRANCES MCDORMAND, Oscar winner (*Fargo*)

"A majority of jobs or at least auditions are gotten via word of mouth. That mouth doesn't open up to an enemy." —PAUL GIAMATTI (*Cinderella Man*)

"Be friendly to everyone, but trust no one. These people are sharks." —KEVIN SPACEY, two-time Oscar winner

"It is crucial to remember, when at an audition, that nobody there wishes you to fail. Everyone wants you to succeed, so they can hire you and go home." —TERRI APPLE, voiceover star

"We casting directors do empathize with actors. Some of us were actors. Truly, we are on your side." —RICHARD PAGANO

"Some stars or producers or whatever treat other people real bad 'cause of all the shit they had to take, coming up. It's like payback time. Only, they pay everyone back, regardless." —SYLVESTER STALLONE

"In Hollywood, everybody says they're your friend. It's your enemies who never declare themselves." —SUE MENGERS, superagent

"Critics aren't our worst enemies. Those are the people who pretend to like us in front of our backs." —EVA GABOR (*Green Acres*)

"Friends are an actor's friends until they become critics." —PETER SELLERS

"I've made enemies, sure. Sometimes not on purpose. But I don't sweat it. I figure I can always get jobs working for the enemies of my enemies." —JOE PESCI (*Goodfellas*)

"If you have not made a single enemy, you are a mediocre actor. If you've made hardly any enemies, you are not a star . . . I'm proud of every enemy I have made." —BETTE DAVIS

"If you are not admired, no one will take the trouble to disapprove." —TRUMAN CAPOTE

"I don't like the word 'enemies.' But I do believe that an ongoing attitude of I'll-show-them can activate and push an actor forward." —BILL MURRAY

"The worst is having to be civil to a slimy, lecherous agent or producer." —HEATHER GRAHAM

"I'll do anything for money. Even associate with my agent." —VINCENT PRICE

"The best way to deflect a horny producer or agent is with firm but polite manners, and with laughter. Laughter can diffuse most situations, even tense or potentially sexual ones." —ELIZABETH HURLEY (*Bedazzled*)

"Learn to laugh at an embarrassing situation, but never at yourself and never at the guy in charge." —ANGELA BASSETT

"Back when Tab [Hunter] and Tony [Perkins] were real close, the story was that Tab told Tony, 'Someday you'll make a fine actor.' And Tony supposedly answered, 'I already have. Several of them.'" —SAL MINEO, two-time Oscar nominee

"The contradiction is when they say an actress has to remain vulnerable, yet to succeed in this business you have to develop the hide of an elephant." —MARILYN MONROE

"I'm tough, ambitious, and I know exactly what I want. If that makes me a bitch, okay." —MADONNA

"Neither a bitch nor a wimp be. That goes for male actors too." —ERIC SHEPARD, International Creative Management agent

"Part of networking successfully is knowing when to ease up. People are more than just connections—there's somebody home there." —JUDITH LIGHT (*Who's the Boss?*)

"We live in a democracy, but we don't work in a democracy. Acting, especially in motion pictures, is very hierarchical, like a caste system. The stars are royalty, the other actors are serfs—okay, commoners. . . . If you're not a big-shot, you gotta be careful not to push or intrude. You gotta watch what you

say, how you say it, and, especially, when you say it."
—BRUCE DERN (*Coming Home*)

"I've been involved with projects where the guys in charge stared when an actress spoke her mind. Not an actor, though—that was expected, that was okay. I'm a friendly person and very proactive, always have been. I have suggestions. As a star or a guest star, I felt entitled to occasionally make some. But boy, one suggestion to the wrong guy and suddenly you're in Siberia." —VALERIE HARPER (*Rhoda*)

"I like to aid in the director's vision. I also like the abrasion that comes about when our visions collide. But I always ache to collaborate." —JAKE GYLLENHAAL

"More than once it was suggested I direct. Because unofficially I did. Sometimes had to! But I didn't seriously consider directing an entire film . . . [because] as actors, we were worked so hard and so often that there wouldn't be time, as there is today, to act and direct. Besides, in those days there was an enormous stigma if you were suspected of being of the lesbian persuasion." —BETTE DAVIS

"If a man puts you on hold, he's busy. If a woman puts you on hold, she's ruthless." —MARLO THOMAS (*That Girl*)

"They talk about divas. You don't hear much about the divos. . . . Nearly all the trouble I've seen caused by a performer was by an actor, not an actress. I'm talking about egos that can erupt into violence and aggression that borders on pathological. . . . On [the set of] *A Man Could Get Killed*, I got into a fistfight with [costar] Anthony Franciosa because he thought stuntmen were beneath him and he wouldn't stop behaving like a turd." —JAMES GARNER

"Some people who become actors are already practically schizophrenic . . . and I've worked with some who were nice in the morning but after lunch they were surly or downright mean. Actors who drank too much lunch, you know?" —ARLENE GOLONKA (*Mayberry, R.F.D.*)

"This one movie-star actress was a major pain in the ass and a phony, so one day I asked her during a break while we were all standing around how long it took her to put on her makeup. She thought I was being impertinent, but I explained my logical assumption that it probably took her twice as long as most actresses because she had two faces." —JACK NICHOLSON

"The only time I ever threw my box-office weight around was on location in Morocco [for Alfred Hitchcock's *The Man Who Knew Too Much*]. The animals there were underfed and treated abominably. I wouldn't speak my lines until the animals on the set were properly fed and watered and handled humanely." —DORIS DAY, founder of The Doris Day Animal League

"Occasionally somebody will say, 'Could you read that line another way?' I just tell 'em, 'I'm sorry, I have no idea how to do that.' It's very rare, and it's not a happy thing." —CHRISTOPHER WALKEN

"Some so-called stars, particularly when it's an inconsequential scene with an 'unimportant' character, don't show up at all, leaving it up to the script supervisor to read their off-camera lines . . . [and] some actors give less of a performance when off-camera, which can create real problems for the actor being filmed.

"Some simply lose focus, but a few are either disinterested or so self-obsessed that nothing matters but their own camera time." —MIKE FARRELL (*M*A*S*H*)

"Burt Lancaster was a huge star, and I had a tiny part in his starring vehicle *The Swimmer*. The plot? He swam from one swimming pool to another—I swear. Anyhow, there I was, thrilled to be participating, and in a scene with Burt himself. He went and did everything he could to try and steal that one little scene. I was so intimidated and so disappointed." —JOAN RIVERS

"Well, Glenn Ford. . . . We were waiting for the camera setup and he was chatting with me. Seemed a nice guy. But once that camera was rolling, he became a total competitor, not acting with me but against me, trying to grab the best camera angle and make any gesture or facial expression that would keep all the attention on himself."
—PAUL FORD, no relation

"On the set with Charlton Heston, a graduate of the Mount Rushmore school of acting. . . . They were setting up, and we'd been sitting side by side, in silence, some twenty minutes. Finally I turn to Chuck and say, 'You know, I just can't sit next to somebody for nearly a half hour and not even say hello.' He turns to me slowly, very condescending, and says, 'Well, I can.'"
—EDWARD G. ROBINSON

"If you want to make sure the camera stays on you and you want to lessen the chance of winding up on the cutting-room floor, stand right next to the star—it's the closest thing to a guarantee that the audience, including your friends and family, will get to see you on the screen." —ROSIE O'DONNELL, after her first movie

"Now and then a movie director chooses a whipping boy to take out his frustrations on. It's painful to watch and listen to, and you usually wonder why the poor shmuck puts up with it. Is it worth

it? No one should put up with that." —JESSICA
CHASTAIN (*Zero Dark Thirty*)

"You notice that when a director or powerful producer chooses someone to pick on, it's never a star.
It's somebody with little or no power that's unlikely
to fight back." —HEATH LEDGER

"I was in a Broadway show where the director was
a bully. To both men and women. When it came
my turn for him to vent his spleen on, I said very
quietly and very forcefully, 'If you ever speak to me
in an uncivil manner, I will hit you over the head
with a chair.' He treated me civilly the rest of the
production." —EDDIE ALBERT (*Green Acres*)

"Remember that the higher the monkey climbs, the
more he shows his ass." —MARTIN SHEEN

"You know what's exciting? Taking part in student
films. Because those young filmmakers are easily
impressed and so appreciative. Not to mention that
several of them will be the big-time directors and
screenwriters of tomorrow. So it's a good way to
make great future contacts." —JERRY MAREN,
former Munchkin

"Be nice, or at least polite, to everyone. Including
secretaries—apt to move up the ladder these days—
and even wives. I only got the part in *Lawrence of*

Arabia because the wife of [director David Lean] was seeing a guru who'd seen me in a silly film role, but felt I should be Lawrence, then told the wife, who agreed to press the issue." —PETER O'TOOLE

"In the States, people typically dress down. You can't always tell if you're talking to someone on the dole [unemployed] or a millionaire. Once, in a New York bar, I sat next to an unshaven man who gave an impression of homelessness. When my friend came in, I excused myself and went to sit with my friend in a booth. He told me that the man I'd been speaking with was a leading movie producer. Incredible! Nor did he have a very wide vocabulary."
—ALAN BATES (*Butley*)

"Schmoozing's a big part of the business. You know who I'd enjoy schmoozing with? The billionaire's daughter who financed *Zero Dark Thirty* and *The Master*. I have a couple of movie ideas I'd like to talk with her about." —ED ASNER

"You never know who has money. They can look like a bum—like a Howard Hughes in disguise. Or they can be 18 and look 16 or 22 and you think they're nobody, but the father's a tycoon. The moral is: be fairly nice to everyone, don't be rude to anyone."
—JESSICA TANDY (*Driving Miss Daisy*)

"It's a fine line between being affable and too nice.

In showbiz, too nice often is seen as weakness. If someone turns out to be important to your career, you can always be nicer to them—as nice as is required. But it's almost impossible to undo rudeness." —LIEV SCHREIBER (*Defiance*)

"How far should you go in being pliable or, uh, cooperative with somebody who can enhance your future? It's better to ponder that and make a decision before it happens, so you can more firmly stick to your own personal and moral guidelines." —RUE MCCLANAHAN (*The Golden Girls*)

"The business is often cutthroat. Hide your vulnerability, don't show your weaknesses. If you expose them, they'll become known, and you can bet there'll be sharks ready to seize on them to try and rip you wide open." —KEVIN SPACEY (*Swimming with Sharks*)

"Don't try to guess who's important and who's not. Treat people decently just because they are people. It's easier to be pleasant to everyone than to wonder who's who and be selectively friendly." —MARY JANE CROFT (*Here's Lucy*)

"There are a few performers who would literally kill for a good part or a surefire vehicle. Just remember: nobody gets out of this life alive, and it's only a movie, it's only a play. And we're not brain surgeons. Also, nothing's surefire." —SYDNEY CHAPLIN, son of Charlie and costar of *Funny Girl* on Broadway

"They call them angels, and they back plays. They put up the money. But you can't always tell they're angels. Forget your mythical stereotypes. You see these guys all over New York, and some are drunks or lechers and dirty old men. But their help can make all the difference in putting you on the stage." —MICHAEL BENNETT, director (*A Chorus Line*)

"We've all read about divas who befriend or at least know by name a movie's key crew members. This sounds delightful, and sometimes it's genuine, but more often than not she's protecting herself against unflattering lighting, bad camera angles, stray hairs, etc. Most relationships in show business are based on advancement and/or self-preservation." —DAVID SHIPMAN, film historian

"In Hollywood, when I entered the set of *Walk on the Wild Side* late once, Barbara Stanwyck, aptly playing a lesbian, tore into me and yelled about my being 'tardy.' Coming from England, I wasn't acquainted with the word.

"The large crew, most of which had worked with her before, were on her side—for some perverse reason they nicknamed her 'Missy'—so I politely held my tongue and acted contrite." —LAURENCE HARVEY

"You can't show up late. It's very, very disrespectful. An actor has to realize when you show up an hour late that 150 people have been scrambling to cover for you. . . . A lot of actors show up late as if they're God's gift to the film, and it's inexcusable and they should have their asses kicked." —WILLIAM H. MACY

"It pays to be on good terms with everybody . . . I've known of impatient movie stars—divas—who throw tantrums in a fitting room, only to have their costumes deliberately taken in a centimeter each day, making them look like barely encased sausages." —RITA MORENO (*West Side Story*)

"Yes, there was the instance of a very cranky director who would yell at the innocent ingénue and one day actually, for no reason known to anyone, slapped her face. You could hear the crew muttering and hissing, and it wasn't long before the director's foot was 'accidentally' broken when a piece of heavy equipment ran over it. I guess these things happen. . . ." —DEBBIE REYNOLDS

"Some directors come on shouting because they want to be known as the person you can't fuck with. . . . But you cannot sustain it for four months or however long the shoot is. Actually, some people can, and it's quite incredible to watch." —DANIEL CRAIG, James Bond #6

"The director's job should be to open the actor up and, for God's sake, leave him alone!" —DUSTIN HOFFMAN

"A good director is like a good psychiatrist. He knows what conclusion he wants you to reach, but he lets you discover it for yourself." —ROD STEIGER

"A destructive director I once had on a movie said to me, 'You're coming off funereal,' instead of just asking for more energy." —CHARLES GRODIN (*The Heartbreak Kid*)

"What are directors if not surrogate parental figures?" —JOHN LEGUIZAMO (*To Wong Foo, Thanks for Everything! Julie Newmar*)

"I was so excited [shooting his first film]. So excited. I was talking to anyone who would listen. After about five days, the director pulled me aside and said, 'Look, stop talking to the crew all day. Just say your lines.'

"It was a serious lesson. You're not on camera for very much of the day. If you're sitting around chatting, it will dissipate a little bit of whatever you've got for when the time comes." —CLIVE OWEN (*Gosford Park*)

"I place no confidence in actors who chatter a lot at rehearsals and do not make notes on planning their homework." —KONSTANTIN STANISLAVSKY

"Between setups, [James Stewart] would disappear from the set. Rather than schmooze with the other actors, he stayed behind closed doors with his assistant, learning his lines, which he had plenty of, and working on his performance. He knew how to use his time better than most of us.

"When he got in front of the camera, he was letter perfect and always knew what he was doing. His acting was so natural that if you turned your back, you couldn't tell if it was Jimmy talking in life or Jimmy talking in the movie." —BEN GAZZARA on his *Anatomy of a Murder* costar

"Don't always judge a star by his cover. What seems like 'aloof' may be shyness, or he might be sparing making you nervous because he's a big star and older, and you're a newcomer with lots on her mind. . . . Stars are often preoccupied, having other concerns—like, they're always wanted for interviews and photos, even on the set." —ANNA PAQUIN, Oscar winner (*The Piano*)

"I'm not the most demonstrative person, even yet . . . I got into acting as a way toward self-expression. Inside a character, I can really let myself go. But when people meet me, it's very possible they think I'm shy or I want to be someplace else." —ROBERT DE NIRO

"As a child, I was lonely and spent a lot of time

in libraries, where no demands were made on one. . . . Acting helped bring me out, it gave me confidence. . . . One of my biggest regrets is that my father didn't live to see my success. He'd have been thrilled—and he wouldn't have believed it."
—MICHAEL CAINE

"I know one iconic Continental actress, still beautiful, used to be the *most* beautiful, who when she goes to the States generally avoids people because so often they stare and they look for, even comment upon, the inevitable flaws of middle age. Where she comes from, people are less obsessed with age and seldom invade her privacy." —DIRK BOGARDE, British star (*Death in Venice*)

"The old saw about 'the bigger they are, the nicer they are' is horse manure, but egos come in all sizes. A few big stars are approachable, and many small and medium stars are as prickly as porcupines. What's nice and saves time is working with somebody you know and like or someone you know has a normal ego, so you can be mutually honest and create and work together uncompetitively." —BEA ARTHUR

"My motto was let everybody shine, because that's the best way to look good." —CAROL BURNETT

"All my life I have been an ensemble actor. It's very nice to be a star, but I passionately believe that a production will be damaged by one egotistical star performance. So I like to create a working atmosphere in which every actor is as important as anybody else, and the work is a community work." —PATRICK STEWART (*Star Trek: The Next Generation*)

"I don't like it when I'm directing when an actor is temperamental. . . . When you do a movie, everybody should leave their personal problems at home. It's difficult enough to make a movie as it is. You don't need extra drama to get it into the can." —ROBERT DE NIRO

"After a couple of weeks of rehearsals, I suddenly found myself having heated arguments with the other actors about a particular moment in a scene, and I realized that I'd stopped being objective about the play and was only seeing it through the eyes of my character." —MICHAEL SHEEN (*The Queen*)

"I could name you two former superstar actresses who were renowned for being bitches on wheels. They could get away with it then. Now older and in the supporting category, they don't even get offered hardly any supporting roles. Their bad habits and reputations caught up with them . . . I didn't say I wouldn't give their initials: F. D. and R. W." —KATHY GRIFFIN, comedian

"As an actor, you don't get excessively close to crew members, who are usually busy anyway. But you shouldn't keep too much of a distance either, especially if you plan someday to direct, when you're less bankable as an actor. That's when you'll definitely need a crew's goodwill."
—BETTY THOMAS (*Hill Street Blues*), who became a movie director (*The Brady Bunch Movie*)

"I remember an actor friend telling me he was happily anticipating working with a writer-director. He said if he had any script questions he'd be able to get all the answers from the director who wrote it. I asked my friend, 'But is it a good script?'"
—ANGELINA JOLIE

"One of the best ways to make productive contacts is via students making films at the university. Some will become the big names of the movie business of tomorrow. If they like you, if you're talented and friendly, they can become lifelong friends or, better yet—I'm being cynical and practical here— associates. Scorsese, Coppola, and others still use some of the actors they met and worked with when they were students." —BRET ADAMS, talent agent

"That saying about being nice to people today who might become VIPs tomorrow is one of the truest pieces of advice for actors. . . . That person billed below you today may in five years be a superstar when you're kind of washed up. If you helped them then, maybe they'll help you tomorrow." —TOBEY MAGUIRE

"Emotions run high in an industry based on duplicating emotion, so there is a tendency to overdo it. Friendships can become too chummy too fast. Real and enduring friendships take time to build—trust is not an overnight thing." —DANIEL MELNICK, producer (*Making Love*)

"There's a maxim my mother was fond of that's particularly applicable to show business: 'Love your friends, love them well. But to your friends no secrets tell. For if your friend becomes your foe, your secrets everyone will know.'" —JODY MCCREA, actor and son of Frances Dee and Joel McCrea

"Verily, the best friend a performer can have is someone who overlooks your failures and tolerates your successes." —ROSIE O'DONNELL

"It's a crying shame, but it's easier to forgive your enemies than to forgive your friends." —MIA FARROW, former partner of Woody Allen

"Confucius or somebody Chinese that wasn't even in show business once advised that you should keep your friends close and your enemies even closer." —TOTIE FIELDS, comedian

"Just because someone keeps calling you 'darling' and 'babe' or 'my man' doesn't mean they mean it. Actors are given to hyperbole, and a newcomer can easily be misled by this." —BENJAMIN BRATT (*The Next Best Thing*)

"The fact is, the Screen Actors Guild does encourage that on-set mistreatment be reported. The truth is, if you make waves, they'll likely boomerang on you. It's a small town, and big egos sometimes come in very small men who have a long and destructive reach. Think twice before making an issue of verbal abuse—physical abuse is a different matter." —JOHN HUGHES, director

"What some insecure directors do is choose a low-billed cast member to pick on or even abuse. They hesitate to pick on a crew member because of those unions' strength. The director's reason for this is to supposedly intimidate everybody else into behaving themselves. Which doesn't exactly help the scapegoat, does it?" —LEONARD FREY (*Fiddler on the Roof*)

"My advice, if you're picked on needlessly and repeatedly by a director, is to nip it in the bud after the third time. But do it privately, just the two of you. If you do it in front of other people, you'll probably make a lifelong enemy of the director." —DOMINICK DUNNE, writer-producer

"Talking about divas, it's not big-name actresses who are the worst. Big-name action actors are often the worst—usually none too bright and highly defensive. As bad or worse are certain directors . . . paranoid types who waited a long time to direct and because directors are now so over-credited believe they're dictators and true artists." —EDMUND PURDOM (*The Egyptian*)

"Things have mostly improved for women in entertainment, though less so for actresses. We're still expected to be grateful we got hired. Today, if an actress coproduces a project, she's allowed her say. But if she's 'only' an actress, she has to be cautiously diplomatic." —BONNIE FRANKLIN (*One Day at a Time*)

"I remember when actresses were widely and belligerently expected to be seen prettily and heard softly and solely in character." —PATRICIA NEAL (*Hud*)

"It's a question of caring whether you're liked or whether you're respected. I'd rather be respected, and am." —BETTE DAVIS

"Billy [Wilder] did have a tendency to call [Marilyn Monroe] 'honey' and other diminutives, and often treated her like a child. I know she resented it, but I guess she was used to it." —JACK LEMMON, on filming *Some Like It Hot*

"He was my manager and then he was my husband and producer . . . rather than argue and have a scene, I gave in and did the projects he wanted."
—DORIS DAY

"From what I've seen of most blonde actresses, I get the impression that the longer they stay blonde, the more their backbone crumbles." —LEE GRAHAM, columnist

"Back in the '30s, almost every new contract player was dyed blonde. No matter how unsuitably. It was meant to put us into a non-individualistic mold that pleased the men, and it was a way of trying to control a studio's actresses. *That* is what came to mind when I saw *The Stepford Wives*!" —BETTE DAVIS

"I had a brunette roommate I didn't get along with because of her conviction that brunettes were naturally smarter. According to her, I was up for sexy roles in frothy—'frothy,' get her!—comedies, while she was so very right for meaty dramatic roles. Anyway, I later received two Academy Awards."
—SHELLEY WINTERS

"Let me tell you, not all the dumbbells in this town are blonde. Or female." —REESE WITHERSPOON

"What's stupid and pointless is making, then keeping, so-called friends who throw cold water on your dreams. This whole endeavor of acting is tough enough without discouragement from those in your personal life." —RACHEL WEISZ (*Agora*)

"Socializing is key to being informed, to getting tips and leads, even booking jobs, and your best sources are other actors. Other actors who are not your same gender, age range, height, weight, and type. . . ." —EDWARD WOODWARD (*The Equalizer*)

"Having a roommate who's also an actress can be great. You both know what each is going through, you can buck each other up, you can pool information, maybe share clothes and shoes, do scenes together, run lines when one gets a part, and so on and so forth." —ANN DORAN (*Rebel Without a Cause*)

"I had a roomie who wanted to be a star. Had the looks, craved the dough and prestige. But he was bone-lazy, wanted someone to discover him. Meanwhile, I was busy coming and going, making contacts, doing this, doing that. Eventually a few minor things started happening for me; he got jealous. One afternoon, sitting by the phone, he sneered at me, 'Mostly you're gonna end up with blisters on your feet.'

"'That,' I said, 'is better than getting them on my ass.'" —TIMOTHY PATRICK MURPHY (*Dallas*)

"A big clue to an actor's personality is when you ask his goal, he says 'star' and bypasses 'actor'. . . . Thousands of clueless hopefuls arrive in L.A. each year, wanting to become 'stars.' Training? No, they got here by car or bus. Patience? No, they don't play cards, and they want everything to happen in six months or less. Pathetic!" —FRANK RIO, agent

"The oddest bad behavior I ever witnessed came from someone I had worked with whom I raved about in print. This guy was deeply offended that I didn't say even more about him." —CHARLES GRODIN (*It's My Turn*)

"Rock Hudson went to see Judith Anderson in *Medea*. He was moved by her extraordinary performance and journeyed backstage to congratulate her. He said, 'I can't tell you how wonderful you were.' She said, 'Try.'" —DALE OLSON, publicist

"As an actor, you have to do occasional reality checks on yourself for the sake of friends and family. Are you always talking about yourself and your work? Do you, even subconsciously, act like you're now more important than most people? This is important, folks!" —JOHN HERBERT, playwright (*Fortune and Men's Eyes*)

"My daughter used to sit and watch *Murder, She Wrote*. I tried to watch with her, but I fell asleep." —ANGELA LANSBURY

"I noticed after going to Hollywood parties with big-name actors and big-name producers [that in] an actor's house the walls were covered with pictures of himself. In a producer's house, the walls were covered with Lautrecs, Van Goghs, and Picassos."
—MICHAEL CAINE

"Actors may have interesting stories to tell, but typically they're not very deep. Their sociocultural range is narrow. You expect it with athletes, like that basketball player who went to Athens and when he came back and was asked if he'd visited the Parthenon said they didn't get to visit any nightclubs. We expect considerably more from actors who can affect our emotions. But most actors need to read more. . . ."
—GORE VIDAL

"There's a line in *The Ladies Who Lunch* where the singer says, 'Perhaps a piece of Mahler's.' I was flabbergasted that Elaine Stritch not only hadn't heard of Mahler but thought Mahler was a food. You're never too old to be disappointed." —GEORGE FURTH, actor-author

"It's rather an amazing fact that one can't necessarily use one's own name as an actor. In the United States, the Screen Actors Guild mandates that you cannot use a name that is already taken, even if it's your own bloody name. My name is James Stewart. Ironically for me, the actor that most people call Jimmy

Stewart anyway was already on SAG's rolls as 'James Stewart.' I was told I could add an initial if I wanted to, but I didn't wish to sound like an accountant."
—STEWART GRANGER, British actor

"There was already an actor named William Macy. He was on [the TV series] *Maude* with Bea Arthur. . . ."
—WILLIAM H. MACY (*Fargo*)

"My friends can call me Roy any time. It's what I went by before I was labeled, for frankly commercial purposes, as Rock. To my fans, it's different . . . they all want a piece of the Rock." —ROCK HUDSON

"If you want to get along with me, please don't say or write that my 'real' name was, you know, whatever my parents chose to name me. My real name is the name that I have chosen. It reflects me far better than a name applied to an infant before she was even born." —EVE ARDEN, *née* Eunice Quedens

"Some Hollywood people are touchy about their names and how to pronounce them. Like, even if they're mispronouncing it, it's their name, so go along with them. If, say, a guy named Weinstein says it's Wine-steen, just call him Mr. Wine-steen. Smarter to stay on their good side." —CARRIE HAMILTON (*Fame*)

"You wouldn't think an unintelligent actor could

convincingly play an intelligent character. However, it's possible if the actor learns the dialogue perfectly and delivers it unhesitatingly. Showbiz is about illusion . . . and sometimes about fraud." —NEIL PATRICK HARRIS (*Doogie Howser, M.D.*)

"I saw a famous actress on *60 Minutes*. 'Cry,' they told her, and she did. Big tears rolled down her cheeks. I will never believe her sincerity again. . . . That has nothing to do with acting." —LIV ULLMANN

"I constantly experience failure in that my work is never as good as I want it to be. So I live with failure. What buoys you up? The people who you have deceived who think you are great and congratulate you on things." —JEREMY IRONS

"They say two actors can't live under the same roof. Correction: two *stars*. Despite their never competing for the same roles. . . . But super-egos clash, and alcohol makes the clashes more frequent and vindictive." —CHEN SAM, publicist to Elizabeth Taylor, who twice married Richard Burton

"Girls, don't date and do not marry an actor. Most of those guys are manic depressive without any chemical condition. They're either raving about their latest part or complaining about the size of the part or their costar or not having a part! Find a nice, uncomplicated businessman. Or make it

big yourself, have affairs, and live happily *sola.*"
—MARIE WINDSOR (*The Narrow Margin*)

"As a lot we moan about not working, and if we get a job we moan about the director, the scripts, and the reviews. If the play's a hit, we then moan about the long run ahead of us. Then we moan because the play closes and we're out of work." —Sir DEREK JACOBI

"Let's be blunt. The worst thing about being an actor is waiting on other people to give you a shot at a good part." —EDWARD NORTON

"It's a very odd relationship acting with someone. You are thrown into a most intimate relationship with a person. Then the picture ends. You may never see the person again. But people say, 'What was he like?' And I don't know. I really don't know them or anything about them." —KATHARINE HEPBURN

"When you first walk on a film set you feel like you've gone to a special place because everybody works very intensely and parties very hard and gets on with each other. . . . On the whole, people are genuinely nice, and you end up with a million phone numbers—a million phone numbers that you don't call. It's kind of sad." —DANIEL CRAIG (*Defiance*)

"The worst is when your first scene together is a so-called love scene. 'Pleasure to meet you. Now let's strip and hop into bed.' Hopefully you're both equally embarrassed. If not, the male should at least have the decency to act embarrassed. . . . It's incumbent upon the director to make you both feel at ease and to provide a dignified working situation. Because it is work, believe me!" —ELIZABETH HURLEY

"The very first day I had this scene where I was supposed to be making out with Michelle Pfeiffer. I told my wife, 'Look, I want you to know that I'm going to be making out with Michelle Pfeiffer today and I'll be thinking about . . . Michelle Pfeiffer.' My wife's response was that when she makes out with me, she also thinks of Michelle Pfeiffer." —PAUL RUDD (*I Love You, Man*)

"Being diplomatic is a recurring aspect of a performer's relationships with others in the field. There was a star actor I'd had a huge crush on when I was new and he was gorgeously middle-aged. But by the time we got to work together, he was old—and in person older than that, if you know what I mean. Somehow, foolishly, I mentioned my youthful crush. That only made it easier for him to propose we . . . get it on—which I no longer had any desire to do.

"Instead of a flat 'no,' I allowed as to how I was flattered by his offer, but now I was so much older than I'd been when I had that crush." —JOAN COLLINS

"To feel good about yourself you should remember what you mean to fans. They put you where you are, and when they stop paying attention, you're on the way down. Unless you retire, you need them. Even then, there's no need for rudeness. As when Joan Crawford married Mr. Pepsi Cola, unaware how soon he'd die and she'd have to resume acting. A little girl asked for Crawford's autograph—too young to know better!—and Joan said something like, 'Go away, little girl, I don't need you anymore.'"
—CESAR ROMERO, the Joker on TV's *Batman*

"One of the greatest moments in my life as an actor came one day outside the Winter Garden Theatre, where I was playing Cassio in *Othello*. It was just after a matinee and I was on my way to lunch when a young man came up to me and said, 'Mr. Grammer, I saw you do *Macbeth* last year, and I want you to know I've been reading Shakespeare ever since.'

"It was one of the most beautiful things I had ever heard. I actually fought back tears. I had never been so proud or so thankful." —KELSEY GRAMMER (*Frasier*)

"Fans can be kinder to a star than your own relatives. Familiarity breeds contempt, you know. . . . My mother was extremely frustrated. She was jealous of my looks. My looks would take me out of the Bronx and directly to Hollywood. . . . My mother once tried to disfigure my face; she was that jeal-

ous and unhappy with her own life and marriage."
—TONY CURTIS

"Would Elizabeth Taylor have become as big a superstar as she did without the many famous men and marriages? I think not. A star, she'd have been. But definitely not as big . . . remember that the pairing of two celebrities doesn't double their publicity, it multiplies it." —JERRY WHEELER, producer

"It doesn't work as well for actors as actresses, but some bodacious beauties try to hurtle toward stardom by becoming or seeming to become romantically and then maritally involved with a male star, prior to the inevitable divorce. And then another male star romance/marriage/divorce. Etc. It can be quite effective." —ERIC SHEPARD, ICM agent

"It was often the case that if a movie wasn't very good, its publicists would try to drum up public interest by pretending the two leads had fallen in love. Nowadays the two leads may concoct a 'relationship' by themselves. And one of them may be gay—or lesbian."
—HERB CAEN, *San Francisco Chronicle* columnist

"Remember when Jodie Foster, who already had two Oscars, was nominated for *Nell?* Her people planted stories that a young man had moved in with her. Several columnists refused to run the item, knowing it to be phony. Well, Jodie didn't win a third Oscar, and later that year the young man came out as gay, which Jodie herself did, long after." —JOE HYAMS, Hollywood columnist

"If you want a marriage that lasts, marry outside the business. If you want lasting friendships, have mostly non-actor friends. And if you want harmonious family relationships, talk as little as you can about your career." —JAMES GANDOLFINI (*Zero Dark Thirty*)

"When it comes to stars, be aware that people like them on the screen or on a stage, but not necessarily in their face. An actor who is popular with everyday people, relatives included, has to be a diplomat." —CLORIS LEACHMAN

"It strikes me as laughable in print interviews when women stars talk about balancing motherhood and a career. What 'balancing'? They have household staff; for example, a housekeeper, a weight trainer, a gardener, a cook, one or two nannies. . . ." —DAVID WATKINS, cinematographer (*Out of Africa*)

"Most movie stars attempt to come across as ordinary people when in fact they're mega-millionaires and get treated like royalty. The only celebrities more deceptive than movie stars are American preachers, who frequently solicit funds for their unholy causes while living in mansions with big staffs and a secret mistress or even boyfriend." —Sir ELTON JOHN

"It's ironic that my brother gets so much publicity, because he doesn't want any publicity. He only wants it for his work. Above all, he doesn't like being stalked and photographed. His bad-boy image is all wrong— he's down to earth and he doesn't act like a star around anyone I know." —CHRIS PENN, actor, on brother Sean

"What bothered me for a long time was that unlike me, my sister [Zsa Zsa] had no interest in acting. But as a famous gossip-column personality, it was she who was offered acting jobs. Her romances and husbands were more helpful to her acting career than the training she never had, but which I did." —EVA GABOR (*Green Acres*)

"Dahling, I never competed with Eva, but every time I would telephone to my mother with news of a new role, she would tell me, 'But did you hear what Eva just did? She got herself a wonderful role in a big new production!' It was our mother's way of making us more competitive with each other. She thought that would make us bigger stars." —ZSA ZSA GABOR (*Moulin Rouge*)

"Things get strained when you have two actors in a family and they're the same sex. That means they're in competition. Almost inevitably there's an estrangement after the younger sibling finds herself or himself in the older one's shadow. Because the elder has the advantage of starting first." —GAVIN LAMBERT, film historian, referencing Natalie and Lana Wood

"Shirley [MacLaine] was willing to costar with her brother once Warren Beatty became a star. Jane and Peter Fonda costarred; they get along fine. But Warren's never asked Shirley . . . apparently he still resents that when he came to [Hollywood] she was already a star and didn't help him out, and he was forced to do TV shows like *Dobie Gillis.*" —KENNY KINGSTON, psychic

"No friction because we brothers are actors. . . . Hey, there's plenty of parts and projects to go around. If there ever was friction, it would more likely be on account of political differences." —ALEC BALDWIN

"All those Baldwin brothers can obtain plenty of work, inasmuch as there are far more film, TV, and stage roles for actors than actresses. If there's more competition between two sisters, it's because there are far fewer female roles going 'round, even for young actresses." —JACKIE COLLINS, actress turned novelist, and Joan's younger sister

"It's funny how in New York the play's writer is often right there and you have to be respectful of the words he's written. You do not arbitrarily change them! But in Hollywood, the writer is seldom around, and even if he is, actors—and I'm talking non-stars—usually feel fine about changing the dialogue. So long as it's okay with the director." —JERRY ORBACH

"The public doesn't know this, but actors soon learn—some the hard way. In movies, the director is the boss. In television, the producer is the boss. Look at the credits on a TV series: the directors come and go and come back, but the producers remain the same." —PETER MARSHALL, host of *Hollywood Squares*

"Actors new to the business sometimes get intimidated by [movie] producers. Many actors are dying to ask them what they actually do, but don't dare. But see, there's less to be intimidated about by a producer. Once filming begins, they're nowhere as busy as directors. They're busiest during pre- and post-production." —CHEVY CHASE

"How to relate to a producer? If he's really big-time, you probably won't even meet him. Some are long-distance, others are hands-on. It varies. They vary. Some are practically kids, some are old men. More and more are women. Most are all right and don't mind being asked questions. Some welcome the attention. Others tend toward pathological shyness." —ALAN BATES (*Zorba the Greek*)

"Producing is the hardest motion picture category to define. A producer may be barely involved, just a money source. Or a producer might be, or try to be, extremely involved—as much as the director allows. Unless of course he's a director-producer. That breed tends to be the most distracted, egotistical, and the hardest to access." —FAYE DUNAWAY

"I once asked a producer how he described his job. He struggled to contain his irritation. He told me it wasn't 'a job.' I asked, 'So what does a producer do?' He raised his chin and sniffed, 'We enable films to be made.' Well, excuuuse me!" —STEVE MARTIN

"Otto Preminger, the director-producer, helped break the censorship code and the political blacklist. So far, so good. But he was also a closet publicist, a would-be P. T. Barnum. Like most directors, he wanted to make a good picture. But while most directors leave it at that, director-producer Preminger wanted his every picture to make a fortune and set records. That led to some tacky decisions . . . [and] he was renowned for mistreating actors, as I well know." —TOM TRYON, actor turned novelist

"Edith Head was her own best publicist. She often insisted on having her photo taken in front of her eight Academy Awards. Mighty impressive . . . when in the presence of icons, the smart thing is to follow their lead. Some like to awe you. Others dislike being treated as institutions. Don't gush, don't be a doormat. Take your cue from them—be no more and no less friendly than they are.

"I'd love to have asked if she knew about the famous graffito EDITH HEAD GIVES GOOD COSTUME. But I instinctually figured she would not have been amused." —SUZANNE PLESHETTE

"Makeup and costume people can be some of the most useful for an actor. They're probably the ones most in the know about what's going on behind the scenes, about the power politics, the delays and why, who's having a crisis and how that affects production, etc., etc." —TED ASHLEY, Warner Bros. executive

"Be sweet to wardrobe . . . makeup too. They directly affect how you look on camera." —CAMERON DIAZ

"People in any specific arena can be shortsighted. They're experts, but not infallible. Like on your costume—before going on the set, check it yourself. Sometimes your fast onceover catches something that the person who was peering at it intently didn't see." —HEATHER LOCKLEAR

"Friendliness can and may happen between you and a star. But friendship? Dream on." —TODD KARNS (*It's a Wonderful Life*)

"Don't try and talk with the cinematographer. Many,

possibly most of them, seem to restrict their on-set relations to their crew and to the director. If you have a question, ask the camera operator instead. I don't think most cinematographers welcome questions from actors, even from stars." —SHELAGH FRASER (*Star Wars*)

"Think twice about any question you want to ask on set. Is it an important question? Logical? Ask something like the size of the shot, so you'll know whether your hands are included. Ask it in a way that tells [the camera operator] you're trying to make his job easier. Because if you use your hands expressively and the director wants to keep that in but the shot was tighter than you thought, then it has to be reshot." —NESTOR ALMENDROS, Oscar-winning cinematographer

"Questions whose answers can be mutually beneficial are the best ones. Questions intended to show off your knowledge are dumb and dumber. Questions designed so you can flirt with someone might be okay if they're not too bold, if you're good-looking or sexy, if you know the person's general tastes, and if nobody overhears." —GUY STOCKWELL, actor-coach

"Cardinal rule: never ask more than two questions of any one person on a set. Always choose an opportune moment. Don't make a habit of asking. You get no points for seeming interested . . . it can even backfire on you." —CHRIS LAMON, stuntman

"If a director gives you a specific direction, repeat it aloud, for your sake and his. Quite often, when he hears it 'played back,' he'll alter or change it. It's peculiar how often directors aren't sure what they want, and how many of them use words they don't really intend. Directors are usually well-prepared on the technical side but often underprepared toward the actors." —FREDERICK COMBS, actor-coach

"Don't sweat it if your director pays little or no attention to you. It's not a slight. No one is busier than a director. They're not focusing on 'I'm making art'; they're more apt to be thinking about budgets, lighting, missing crew members, script rewrites, deadlines, a hundred things. If a director smiles at you, take it as a big compliment." —SHIRLEY MACLAINE

"Some directors pay you little heed because they like what you're doing but aren't the type to say so or because they don't know what they want and will therefore make you do retakes until they see what they want—something that they weren't able to put into words. Not all directors are articulate. Especially the majority that aren't writers." —STANLEY GREENBERG, screenwriter (*Soylent Green*)

"I said to him, 'Hitch, you never tell actors what to do. You set up the scene, we know our blocking, we come in, we do the scene, and you never tell us what you expect from the scene.'

"He said, 'Karl, I am a professional. And I hope that I have hired professionals. We all do our jobs and we go on from there.'" —KARL MALDEN, on making *I Confess* with Alfred Hitchcock

"The worst experience I ever had with a director came from a man who never screamed, wasn't a bully, in fact was a very sweet guy. The problem was, he directed too much. 'Turn at the door and smile. Do that thing you do with your eyes, I love that.'

"'What do you mean? What thing?'

"'You know, that thing you do.' 'Reach out on this word.' 'Stress this word.' 'Say it like this.' And what felt like 67,000 other directions. This guy was reducing good actors to good puppets. Ironically, he's very successful."—CHARLES GRODIN (*Beethoven*)

"I'm lucky because I'm inventive. I'm spontaneous and combustible, and I prefer change over sticking to a pattern—which can be a creative challenge during a long theater run. . . . So when Jerome Robbins clearly didn't know what the hell he wanted in *Fiddler on the Roof*, I simply kept giving him variations and brand-new stuff until he saw something he liked. Not a very good director, but not a problem for me." —ZERO MOSTEL

"You have to be careful with directors, less in what you say to them than how you say it. I was on location with a director who was fond of wrapping ahead of time. He kept rushing us, me in particular. Finally, I stopped, grinned, and calmly told him, 'They give awards for good acting, not for fast acting.' He got and accepted the message, and I later got congratulations from the cast and some crew members." —HEATH LEDGER, Oscar winner

"Shouting at a director, no matter how warranted— and it often is!—is purely detrimental. Unless you are the star." —ED ASNER

"Before you open your mouth to complain, examine the situation from the other's point of view. Always. Show business is a small community. People in it have long memories. If you burn your bridges in Hollywood and New York, there are no other major places you can work at your trade—excuse me, craft." —ROBERT YOUNG (*Father Knows Best*)

"It's a fine line actors must walk in their professional relationships. One side of the coin requires you to be highly confident, even inwardly arrogant—'arrogant' literally means claiming for oneself . . . claiming your right to be there, your right to perform, and to be treated properly.

"The other side of the coin is that so often you must defer to your bosses, of whom there seem to be so many, and you must be civil, at least, to your coworkers, and more than civil to coworkers much more successful than you, because in a way they're your bosses too—that is, a star can get you fired." —SUSAN STRASBERG (*Picnic*), daughter of Lee

"One of the most useless, timewasting things young actors tend to do is when they have a complaint and repeat it to most anybody except the party they're complaining about. Occasionally using a friend to let off steam is one thing. But being upset with A and telling B, C, D, and E about it only perpetuates discontent. And changes absolutely nothing." —MARY WICKES, character actress (*White Christmas*)

"Romantic relationships can be based on feelings. Professional ones shouldn't be. Use logic. Think of the long run. Don't try and abuse a friendship or relationship; it'll come back to haunt you. Be positive, not negative. Don't hold onto grudges. There—that's my time-tested advice." —CLINT EASTWOOD

"'Civilian' friends can't hurt your career. Industry friends and associates can. Kiss and make up, or anyway shake hands. Who needs the aggravation? You'll sleep better and your career will go smoother." —ADRIEN BRODY (*The Pianist*)

"Charles Lang, the famous cinematographer, said when he worked in France principal members of the crew would shake hands every morning on set, regardless of what happened the previous day. Why can't *we* do that?" —LOUIS EDMONDS (*Dark Shadows*)

"Once in a while, admit you're wrong. It's no crime, and you'll be admired. So long as you're not wrong too often." —CATHERINE ZETA-JONES

"There's more to show business than acting. The limitations are your own. I was an actor until I was 35. I didn't feel the connection with acting anymore. . . . So I decided to stop. I wanted to produce, for films or TV. Was I determined? I wrote letters, contacted everyone I knew, made use of all the connections I'd built up. Six weeks later, I got my first producing job." —JOSEPH STERN, *Law & Order* producer

4

WORKING

"First rule for the working actor is read your contract. The word 'contract' begins with 'con.'" —SUSAN STRASBERG (*Stage Struck*)

"Two specialized reading skills an actor requires: reading scripts for subtext, and reading contracts for your future. A lawyer or agent may read your contract, but you should too. The agent or lawyer can't always be trusted, especially the lawyer." —SUZANNE PLESHETTE (*The Bob Newhart Show*)

"How do you get better at reading contracts? Same way you get better at acting and everything else—by doing it over and over . . . experience. Someday you'll look back and think, *Why was I so intimidated?* Meanwhile, you may have saved yourself untold dollars and hassles." —ROBERT E. LEE, playwright (*Inherit the Wind*)

"Reading a contract may look daunting at first. They are long and the sentences are involved. Those sentences are decipherable, though—look for the *verbs*. This is something you ought to learn to do for yourself. *How?* Read sample contracts. Read a book on contracts—*Contracts for Dummies* or whatever. Go to a law library and browse and ask questions. Take a junior-college law course.

"We're talking about your own well-being. In this business, the sole person you can totally trust is yourself—and if you're chemically dependent, sometimes not even." —PATRICK SWAYZE

"Managers and business managers can pull the rug out from under your feet. Sweethearts like Doris Day and tough guys like Kirk Douglas have been bilked of millions by theirs—by men they once trusted implicitly." —ESTELLE GETTY (*The Golden Girls*)

"It's not a good idea for an actress to allow her husband to manage her career. An acting career should last a lifetime. Most show-business marriages do not. . . . There's also the excessively pro-male law whereby a wife cannot testify against her husband, even if he's taken her for everything she's worth." —DOROTHY MANNERS, columnist

"Do not blithely assign power of attorney to anyone in your professional life. Don't give anybody such a degree of control. There are stories galore of stars who were swindled by remaining ignorant of their finances—and even more unpublicized stories of non-stars who got swindled and couldn't recoup their monies the way a star eventually could. Get in charge of your own workings!" —DAWN STEEL, head of Columbia Pictures

"Years ago, people advised me to have a business manager. Coincidentally, a lawyer who worked at my agency was leaving to become a business manager. So I relaxed—I would have a friend handling my financial affairs. . . . Things went well, I made lots of money. Sam Norton, my business manager, gave me financial reports that I didn't understand, and papers to sign. I signed away everything until I was broke." —KIRK DOUGLAS

"A woman trusts her husband. . . . Sometimes trust is not warranted." —DORIS DAY, whose husband-agent and his business partner lost over $20 million of her money

"An actor is a corporation of one. You are your product, and you are the president of your company. If you value yourself, act responsibly and judiciously! If you need to look up 'judiciously,' do so." —GEORGE SIDNEY, director (*Show Boat*)

"The more actors know about the world—the more knowledge they have—the better actors they can be." —STELLA ADLER, acting coach

"Silence is golden, but learning is priceless, and a good actor never stops learning." —MARIA OUSPENSKAYA, actress-coach

"There's a reason actors have a rep for not being too bright. Not just that most don't go to college . . . so many are self-limited. All they think and care to know about is themselves. They may be more into imagination than reality, and ambition may keep them from looking outward, from learning." —CHARLIE EARLE, publicist

"I used to think directors were automatically smarter than actors. Now I know there are egregious exceptions. Once, after a trip to Bali, a director asked me if I'd gone to Bali Hai. He wasn't smiling; he was in earnest. So I tactfully chose not to answer, 'I didn't even go to Bali Junior High.'" —MARIAN MERCER (*Nine to Five*)

"Shangri-La, Bali Hai, and so forth are fictional places. They're from fiction that Hollywood filmed. If the average moviegoer thinks they exist, that's one thing. But when highly paid people out of Hollywood think they're real . . . that's sad. It's too easy to become cocooned in an ignorant, two-dimensional world of only make-believe and money." —JOSEPH PAPP, stage producer

"You know what is beyond stupid? Gay actors who

join a homophobic cult cum religion to hide behind. Even with legally attached wives, the truth eventually starts leaking out. Even stupider? Gay stars who continually come on to *straight* masseurs and caterers, etc., and keep landing in the tabloids and getting threatened with lawsuits. . . . But isn't self-hate a hallmark of stupidity?" —DALE OLSON, publicist

"If you want to be an actor and are a writer, keep that under your hat. Writing scares a lot of people who don't do it, and directors will think you'll want to rewrite your dialogue. If you've written a book, keep that especially quiet. A screenplay you can get away with, but books intimidate movie people. Unless they've bought the screen rights to yours, in which case they'll be delighted to mangle it into unrecognizable shape." —MICHAEL MCDOWELL, screenwriter (*Beetlejuice*)

"Instead of ever reading a book, too often an actor will say, 'Hey, I should write a screenplay I can, like, star in.'" —OLIVIA GOLDSMITH, author (*The First Wives Club*)

"I'm sorry, but I have to unload here. The more often you use the word 'like' when it doesn't mean 'to be fond of,' the more stupid you will sound. Like, have I made my point?" —SUE MENGERS, agent

"This awful, mindless habit . . . saying 'like' so needlessly, so often, undercuts what you're saying. It makes it sound as if you're not sure. . . . When 'like' turns up in every sentence, or even more than once per sentence, the impression, basically, is that you're a moron."
—RICHARD WIDMARK, former schoolteacher

"I've known actors of both genders who remove their glasses before walking onto a set. They think glasses interfere with their looks or appeal. Obviously, if a role doesn't call for wearing glasses, and most roles don't, then before you go into makeup the glasses will come off. But why prematurely dumb yourself down?" —COLIN HIGGINS, screenwriter-director and author of *Harold and Maude*'s screenplay

"Don't come onto my set chewing gum. I mean, how dumb is that?" —HOWARD ZIEFF, director (*Private Benjamin*)

"Truly, is one here to work or to have a good time on someone else's money? My estimation of an actor plummets if he or she comes into work chewing gum or texting, talking on a cell phone, etc. I have more and better things to do than play schoolmaster to immature nonprofessionals." —KEN LOACH, U.K. director (*Kes*)

"Don't come in wired up and plugged in and listening to music or whatever. Your dialogue should be what's in

and on your mind. Don't distract yourself and us with gadgets and paraphernalia unconnected to the job."
—DANIEL MELNICK, producer (*Footloose*)

"Actors cannot afford to be distracted or have an attention-span deficit. Acting in front of a camera or a live audience requires intense concentration, to shut out the real world and create the character's reality. Focus is just as important for an actor as for a cinematographer." —KEIRA KNIGHTLEY

"I'm the only actor in my family . . . I love them, but if they're in the audience when I'm in a play, I'd rather not know. It kills make-believe for me. I'm more comfortable making believe in front of complete strangers or other actors." —GLENDA JACKSON, two-time Oscar winner and MP [Member of Parliament]

"You can become like a family, in some working situations. But that's relatively rare, excuse the pun. Most of the time, there's too little time for socializing. It really is about the work." —GEORGE CLOONEY

"I know some younger people, especially ones newer to the industry, like to 'hang out' or just 'hang,' want to chat with cast and crew, especially crew, to show how democratic they are. Problem is, everyone has a job to do, and too much chat gets in the way." —JOHN MALKOVICH (*Places in the Heart*)

"Being a professional means getting there on time, being prepared, and not taking up everyone else's time."
—QUENTIN TARANTINO

"Noel Coward and then Spencer Tracy were famous for saying that an actor should always show up on time, know his lines, and not bump into the furniture. However, Stanislavski said the same thing, and before them." —GALE SONDERGAARD, first Best Supporting Actress Oscar winner

"Punctuality is the basis. The foundation. Without it, the most gifted actor on earth is worthless."
—RICHARD THORPE, MGM director

"Marilyn Monroe was never on time, never knew her lines. I have an old aunt in Vienna. She would be on the set every morning at six and would know her lines backward. But who would go to see her?" —BILLY WILDER, writer-director (*The Seven Year Itch*)

"A star can get away with such inappropriate behavior as being late or indulging in a tantrum. So long as it doesn't become a habit or cost the studio too much money. But until you are a star, don't do such things. Or you'll never get to be a star." —DAVID LEWIS, producer (*Camille*)

"It's a true story. Burt Reynolds told it in his memoirs. The day Joan Crawford died, he was at a party. Bette

Davis enters the room, goes up to Burt and the man he's talking to. She lights a cigarette and tells Burt, 'Did you hear? The bitch died today.' Immediately Burt says, 'Miss Davis, this is a gentleman of the press. . . .'

"To whom Bette immediately turns, smiles, and adds, 'But she was *always* on time.'" —RON VAWTER (*Philadelphia*)

"It's so easy to gossip among fellow actors. Sometimes simply to relieve tension or become cozy or [be] an insider. We all love to hear dish. But the wiser policy is to avoid it. If you badmouth someone, the person listening will likely wonder, *Would he say something similar about me if I wasn't here?* Eventually, people who badmouth others get a bad reputation and are shied away from." —JACK ALBERTSON (*Willie Wonka and the Chocolate Factory*)

"Avoid negativity and negative people like the plague! In this world of showbiz, there's enough that can and will go wrong that you *need* an upbeat outlook. . . . Hanging around with negative people and losers will, in the end, only make you negative and a loser." —JOHN LARROQUETTE (*Night Court*)

"The little things mean a lot. A smile or kind word, a sincere inquiry into how someone's holding up . . . that sort of thing. Little courtesies make working together

smoother and get people on your side. Including people who can help you or make you look good."
—CAROL BURNETT

"Some cold people who become actors learn to relate only to characters. But this is a social business, a people business. You have to connect with real people, not just characters. Occasionally you should be nice out of character. It also helps your career last longer."
—SCARLETT JOHANSSON

"Successful actors, meaning those with a range, not necessarily those who own a mountain range in Montana, have the ability to turn passion into compassion. Even a villain should be able to feel and demonstrate pity." —ALAN BATES (*A Day in the Death of Joe Egg*)

"The great gift of human beings is that we have empathy. We can all cry for each other and sense a mysterious connection to each other. If there's hope for the future of us all, it lies in that. And it happens that actors can evoke that event between hearts."
—MERYL STREEP

"We were on location doing the story of Matthew Shepard, the gay youth who was tortured to death in Wyoming. Stockard Channing and I were playing his parents. When we got out of the car in the scene and I looked at Stockard, I was stunned . . . her face was the picture of utter grief, it was so real and devastating. It really impacted me, and it heightened my own reaction as the father." —MARTIN SHEEN

"It's in the eyes, mostly. Don't listen just to the other actor's lines. Look at—and listen to—their eyes. That's where the emotion comes through." —CHARLIZE THERON

"To listen involves being silent. But you know, some people are afraid of the silences between words or statements. Yet the silences enable accuracy or eloquence or deep emotion to percolate and rise to the surface." —ROY SCHEIDER (*Jaws*)

"The best advice on relating to others as a person or an actor is to *listen*. To be a sponge, you must absorb. If you'd rather talk or expound, go into politics or preaching. Which these days are often the same thing." —SUSAN SARANDON

"The rudest thing an actor can do, as an actor and as a person, on or off the set, is to not pay attention. To not listen. That is so dismissive." —ADAM SANDLER

"When you're new to acting, you'll get tripped up now and again by thinking you must be that character, must change yourself into that person. No. You are, you appear as yourself—you can't change your body—but your words and reactions are those of the character, as supplied by the writer and perhaps modulated by the director. Eventually you realize it doesn't have to be that complicated." —JAMES LEO HERLIHY, playwright (*Blue Denim*)

"[Director Philippe] Garrel used to say to me, 'Don't think about acting. Just be in the character's thoughts, be simple. Her thoughts are enough. If you're thinking right, you'll be all right.'" —CATHERINE DENEUVE

"The way I see it, if the actor's instincts are against the grain of the director's, then the director cast the wrong guy. The director has got to support the instincts of the actor, every time. You can compromise and fit the director's mold, but the spark of spontaneity will be gone." —SEAN PENN

"No names, please, but when you direct a star who is more star than actor, your job becomes difficult, technically and emotionally. You're quite aware that you're directing a commodity, a brand intended to fill the seats. . . . Hopefully the star's dialogue and looks or personality, plus the other actors and characters, the movie's plot, its pace and suspense, etc., will overcome your star's limitations. But not always.

"If the movie flops, you're despondent and disgusted. If it's a hit, you're delighted, somewhat surprised, and only semi-disgusted—secretly—with yourself. And if it is a hit, you may very well work with that untalented *shlub* again!" —JOHN HUGHES (*Home Alone*)

"With a not-so-good or lousy actor, you still have to react like he's a good actor. Don't descend to his level. That's an easy trap to fall into. Do your best, and try not to work with him again." —KATE HUDSON (*Almost Famous*)

"Some actors give you so little in a scene. There's a myriad of reasons . . . some actors are just attractive facades—maybe there's no *there* there, like Oakland. Some have little or no imagination, only got into acting for money and fame. Some are emotionally constipated. Truth is, a lot of actors should never have become actors. You can only hope they'll get better with time." —DREW BARRYMORE

"Working with someone real famous who isn't versatile like Meryl Streep or most English actors can be a drag. On account of they're locked into portraying themselves over and over. They don't vary; they're afraid if they do they'll disappoint audiences and they'll stop coming. These stars no longer view themselves as actors, but as icons or institutions. Which is death to creativity." —RICHARD DREYFUSS

"Rehearsal is so valuable, because then you can experiment. You and your director can evolve your character together. But other than on the stage,

there's less and less rehearsal—too expensive in terms of time. This is probably the biggest reason true actors, those who love to explore character and get it right, return to the stage for very little money compared to what they earn for films and television."
—LINDA LAVIN, Broadway star, aka TV's "Alice"

"If you ever get the luxury of rehearsal, which a few movie directors will contractually insist on, use it! It can make the difference between a competent performance and an Oscar nomination, to be crass about it." —TILDA SWINTON, Oscar winner (*Michael Clayton*)

"Don't be afraid to make mistakes in rehearsal—which is what it's for. It's the time to try and go 'too far,' which might not be too far, could be just right for the character and riveting to watch. You'll never know if you don't put it out there." —CHRISTOPHER REEVE

"In plays you act in sequence, in movies practically never. What's wise and safer is to know all your scenes before filming. Not every word, necessarily, but most of them, and the gist of the scene and its relevance to the overall plot. Because fairly often, you'll come to work prepared with that day's scheduled scene, and if at the last minute it's replaced with another scene, you'll have to memorize and act it with maybe an hour's notice." —WILLIAM BELASCO, agent

"A movie set can be a scary place, but a TV set can be terrifying. If a movie runs over budget or over schedule, well, that can happen—then they cut you some slack. But for TV, it has to be in the can for airing next week. Maybe they go over budget, but they cannot go over schedule, or else!" —CHARLIE HUNNAM (*Pacific Rim*)

"It's a bit of a farce to think the better actors are in motion pictures, while the lesser ones are on telly. I speak, *ahem*, as a movie star and impartial observer. For the small screen, owing to time constraints, rehearsal is nil. Those who get hired are the ones who can deliver finished performances at an audition. Those of us who take a bit more time to 'find' and refine the character, we're selected for the movies, where we have a bit more time and the director can actually take a few minutes to coach us." —HUGH GRANT (*Maurice*)

"In England an actor is an actor is an actor, and since most of their work is done in London, actors can do TV in the morning, a film job in the afternoon, and end with a stage role that night. But in the U.S.A., with our peculiar geography, we're stuck with those built-in prejudices. There are some actors who excel in all three areas, but we must repeatedly break down those prejudiced walls to prove it." —RUE MCCLANAHAN (*The Golden Girls*)

"One thing I have to call the U.S. on is their conflating the character with the actor. . . . So many American actors fear playing a gay character lest it reflect on them. Yet they don't hesitate to play a murderer—often. In England and the rest of Europe, gay people are part of life, and of course one is going to be offered gay roles, and if the script is good, one accepts. 'Big deal,' as I think they say in Peoria." —MICHAEL YORK (*Cabaret*)

"I played gay once [on Broadway in the musical *La Cage aux Folles*]. Just once. I'm straight." —GENE BARRY, born Eugene Klass

"I did a foreword to the memoir by [MGM hairdresser] Sydney Guilaroff. I was told he 'came out' in it as Jewish, but that he didn't acknowledge being gay. That's his choice, but it does seem rather inappropriate." —ANGELA LANSBURY, who admitted her first husband was a gay actor

"Long ago, I had to work with an actor I didn't like. Not because he was gay, which he was, but his need to . . . he was just obnoxious. As some actors can be. But this one wasn't part-time. Anyway, to some degree it affected our professional interaction. Today, I wouldn't allow it to do so. One acquires discipline." —COLIN FIRTH (*The King's Speech*)

"Don't ever forget that acting is interacting. It's two of

you, sometimes more. It's never a monologue, except in auditions or maybe Shakespeare." —K CALLAN, actress-author

"It shouldn't be called acting. It should be called reacting. And to react truthfully, you have to listen. That's not as easy as it sounds, because in everyday life we only half listen. In reacting, we have to listen fully, for extended stretches. It's a necessary skill good actors need to learn. It comes with experience and being consciously in the moment." —MAUREEN STAPLETON, Oscar winner (*Reds*)

"Learn your lines, certainly, but don't over-rehearse or over-plan. That can erase spontaneity. You'll need spontaneity if you're in a play, night after night, or before the camera, take after take." —RACHEL WEISZ, Oscar winner (*The Whistle Blower*)

"Possibly the greatest-ever American stage performance was Laurette Taylor's in *The Glass Menagerie*. Ask anyone who saw that legendary performance. The reason? Every time she performed it, it sounded like she was saying the lines for the very first time. Each time, she lived it anew." —PAUL NEWMAN, who directed a film version of Tennessee Williams's play

"Believability is freshness is spontaneity. It derives from your acting in the moment. This is done by believing completely in the circumstances and words and goals of your character, and by listening avidly to whoever is speaking to you.

"Of course, keen listening doesn't mean staring at who's speaking. As in real life, one sometimes looks away . . . one sometimes measures the words spoken to one; maybe one plots and schemes while listening. But you live the character's life, and it's all unfolding for the first time, whether it's your sixtieth performance or your sixth take." —NINA FOCH, actor-coach

"An acting class won't give you talent. It will, or should, give you technique. That's what you need over the long haul. Inspiration can't be relied upon. Technique can." —BRADLEY COOPER (*Silver Linings Playbook*)

"Hopefully your acting teacher didn't direct you, but truly taught you. In other words, she or he didn't just tell you how to do a scene better, but instead taught you to decide whether a scene needs to be better and how to judge for yourself how to improve it. Because once you're on set, you're on your own. Directors don't have time to teach or give tips. They want results, and fast. In this business, time is money." —MIRA SORVINO (*The Great Gatsby*)

"An actor shouldn't ask me what his motivation is. That is an actorly concern, one he should have

worked out for himself before we commence a scene."
—ROBERT ALDRICH, director (*What Ever Happened to Baby Jane?*)

"It bothers me when a star needs handholding. No matter how pretty she is, if it's a she. If I do that, the other actors resent it, and rightfully so. But don't blame the director—stars have to be pampered, not, unfortunately, kicked in the ass." —SAMUEL FULLER, director (*The Big Red One*)

"One actor asked me after a take if he was being villainous enough, which astonished me, because his lines were boldly sadistic. I told him, 'You don't really need to play a villain or a hero. Your script does it for you. You just say the words convincingly, and you're the villain.'" —SIDNEY LUMET, director (*Twelve Angry Men*)

"Simply presenting text effectively—that's all acting is." —BARRY PINEO, acting coach and author (*Acting That Matters*)

"Actors will expect me to direct them through a scene. But they've been employed on the understanding that they are trained and know how to perform a scene by themselves. I only have a word with an actor if he has not performed adequately. When actors perform well, I assume they're intelligent enough to know it too." —ALFRED HITCHCOCK

"I thought Mr. Hitchcock was disappointed in me. He didn't talk to me or encourage me . . . nothing. Some time into shooting, I learned that the reason he hadn't said anything was he liked what I did." —DORIS DAY

"You'll meet every kind of director in this business. The traffic cops. The ones who want to play your role for you. The ones who are fatherly and helpful. The miserable bastards on power trips. The ones who ignore everyone but the two stars—and try to sleep with one, or both, of 'em! Eventually you'll work with them all. It's gonna be some trip!" —BEN STILLER

"Lots of directors aren't sure what they want from an actor. Or they can't articulate it, unless they're also writers. They'll make you do take after take until they see something they do like. Meanwhile, they can't tell you what they want because they don't always know what they want. Not that they'll admit it. So it's up to the actor to supply the goods, and lots of 'em!" —BRAD PITT

"I know it was her first time directing, but Nancy Walker wasn't right for the job (on *Can't Stop the Music*). You wouldn't believe how many takes we did of my reading of a simple two-or-three-word line—don't even ask. I had done every possible combination of saying those words, and then some. Finally I had to say, 'That's it!

Let us move on.' Somebody had to be willing to say it."
—VALERIE PERRINE

"Be patient with your director. Besides being in his hands artistically, your movie, or any movie, is a work in progress. Scripts often get revised, so do the ideas in a director's head. He may be coming up with new and better ones. If you have one or two to contribute, find the right time and place and perhaps some privacy. Apart from that, please be patient." —ROBERT ALTMAN, director

"I asked a director I met socially why he gave up acting. He explained that once his hair was gone and he was past 30, he wouldn't be a lead. Maybe he never heard of hairpieces, or wouldn't want to wear one. He said he'd rather be a leading director than a non-leading man. I wouldn't have guessed he had such ego. On the other hand, I suppose being a director requires a fairly massive ego." —EILEEN BRENNAN (*Private Benjamin*)

"A number of directors were once actors. Some were and still are good actors and can hide their fear well."
—MICHELLE YEOH (*Tomorrow Never Dies*)

"The best time to complain about on-set goings-on or the lack of them is after a film wraps. Then, the whinging [sic] can't hurt the project. But don't complain on set, and if another actor badmouths the director or other actors, ignore him. They used to say loose lips sink ships. At any rate, they don't help the smooth progress of filming any." —LESLIE GRADE, agent

"Costarring with Bruce Willis? He was new to the big-time [on *Moonlighting*]. It went to his head. More, I cannot possibly say, and you could not possibly have time to hear it all." —CYBILL SHEPHERD

"Apparently when someone is on drugs, they're quiet or sleepy. When I worked with Robert Downey, Jr. [in *Restoration*] his well-known drug escapades were evidently a thing of the past. Unfortunately for working conditions. Talk about wanting to be the center of attention...." —HUGH GRANT

"When your coworker is disruptive, it finally gets tempting to try and put him in his place. But as a fellow actor, that's difficult. It's also not really your place, and it can backfire. Mostly, you have to grin and bear it. Leave it up to the director or other authority figure. Unlike in 'real' life, it's best not to get involved." —BARBARA EDEN, teamed with troublesome Larry Hagman in *I Dream of Jeannie*

"It may help to think of a set as a classroom. There are all you students—the actors—and there is one teacher—the director. If another student acts up, excusing the expression, you do not take sides. You keep

your nose clean and leave the discipline to teacher."
—HAYDEN RORKE (*I Dream of Jeannie*)

"One doesn't usually want to be an egotist, but when you're working, you really must focus and zero in on your reactions. I hear very little out of one ear, but my other ear is really good, and that's all I need! But I really have to concentrate." —JANE LYNCH (*Glee*)

"I've learned so much from the animals. . . . One thing I learned early on, during acting, is to watch your scene partner like a dog watches—fully and focused and ready." —BETTY WHITE

"While on set, you learn to sharpen your senses. What exactly are you seeing, listening to and hearing; what's really going on? Among the crew, and then, when the camera rolls, among the actors, specifically, those you're supposed to react to."
—RON PALILLO (*Welcome Back, Kotter*)

"It's not about tension, though it may seem like it at first. It's about acute observation. The more you notice, the more you absorb and the more you can emit. If you skim the surface of your surroundings and relationships, more than likely your on-camera result will be shallow too." —CHARLES LAUGHTON

"Don't look at the set as a set. Look at it as a place—

your place. The place you're currently living in or passing through. Feel like you belong. Isn't that all acting is? Feeling. . . ." —GENA ROWLANDS

"Sometimes I still get nervous on a set—after dozens of pictures! I often feel like I gotta keep moving, if only for a protective device." —TONY CURTIS

"The great Vietnamese monk and meditation master Thich Nhat Hanh once challenged the restless, automatic Western attitude of 'Don't just sit there; do something!' with, 'Don't just do something; sit there!' For there is a largely untapped world inside. . . ." —PETER COYOTE (*Outrageous Fortune*)

"An excellent, progressive German novelist, Hermann Broch, said that doubt gives rise to discontent. Reading that helped me as an actor. It let me increase my inner stillness, which looked to others like confidence. . . . When they reacted to me as if I were more confident, I became more confident." —CURT JURGENS, German actor (*The Spy Who Loved Me*)

"We used to resemble each other when younger, and I once heard myself referred to—not in print, of course—as 'a heterosexual Cary Grant.' Of course as a leading man I deliberately shunned comparisons. We're each supposed to be unique . . . I relaxed a bit after my Academy Award [Grant never won one]. Had

I kept my original name, I'd have been too unique. For Hollywood." —RAY MILLAND (*The Lost Weekend*), fellow Englishman, *né* Reginald Truscott-Jones

"Make your mind into an ally. In the thespic art, the mind is more crucial than in any other." —EVA LE GALLIENNE, actor-producer-coach

"'Panic' comes from the Greek demigod Pan. 'Pan' means 'across' and 'all.' All actors experience some degree of panic, including stage fright, at some time. It comes from wanting to do well and being afraid not to. It can be channeled into feelings because it already is *feeling*. Intense feeling. Believe me, a panicky or stage-frightened actor is far more interesting to watch than one who blithely sails through and doesn't much care." —JOSHUA LOGAN, director (*South Pacific*)

"I have never really gotten over stage fright. The saving grace is that it's something which occurs before you perform. Once the performance is underway, the stage fright is either forgotten or it hovers at the edge of your mind, just enough to keep you on your toes." —HELEN HAYES, stage star and two-time Oscar winner

"You know how there are people who are worriers and some who aren't, or who don't worry a lot? The same among actors. There will always be those who worry too much, too often, and too long. It's not that they're better or more concerned, they're just natural worriers. The rest of us are concerned, are good, but we don't worry excessively." —ERIC PORTMAN, British actor (*The Whisperers*)

"Don't sweat the little stuff . . . I was in a play where one of the leads became near-obsessed with the amount of cutlery on the table during a dinner scene. What did it matter? All he had to use was one fork and one knife. The rest was basically decoration." —CHRISTOPHER REEVE

"I was on location, somewhere in an in-between [American] state. The second-unit director was unknown to me. It was early morning, there was dew on the flowers in the field, and the second-unit director commented upon what he called *daffy-dils*. I had to stifle an urge to telephone the director back in Hollywood and ask whether this man was qualified for this job. After all, it was a major production." —LAURENCE HARVEY (*The Manchurian Candidate*)

"Some performers have quirks that some directors do nothing about. Now, I don't happen to think any actor is irreplaceable . . . I recall hearing about Ed Begley, a good but stubborn and rascally actor. Oscar or no Oscar, I would have disciplined or replaced him. He appeared in a forgettable play where each night he did an unforgettable and unforgivable thing. He had a line with the word 'Katmandu' [the capital of Nepal] in it, but when he came to that word, Begley would break into a little song and dance with, 'Oh, the cat woman can't, but the cat man do.' Every single night!" —JOSE QUINTERO, stage and film director

"I'd considered acting as a career but hated the idea of being shouted at by both the director and the leads. By the director alone, perhaps. In any case, I went into editing, and in England the directorial style is, or was, quite gentlemanly, so I got along with my directors . . . and in time got to direct. Seldom did I yell at anybody, although to be perfectly honest, when I did it was well deserved and I rather enjoyed it." —PETER HUNT, who helmed the first Bond movie without Sean Connery, *On Her Majesty's Secret Service*

"Do you know, sometimes a very effective actor or theme is resented by some audience members precisely because they were emotionally moved? These are people who may rarely be moved, whose home lives are static, and then they go to the theater and are unprepared for or used to emotion hitting them in the face or gut. But instead of being grateful, these men— they generally are men—resent it! A few of them have written aggravated letters to myself or to actors in my plays." —SHELAGH DELANEY, playwright (*A Taste of Honey*)

"Humans have a tendency to blame, to point the finger. The problem with blame is that it's really an

acknowledgment that someone else is in charge and you're powerless—that the other is stronger than you. When you blame, you're empowering someone else."
—JOHN CAZALE (*Dog Day Afternoon*)

"Blame and blaming don't solve any problems. They just further you away from the solution." —RAY BRADBURY, writer (*Fahrenheit 451*)

"When you complain about what someone else did to you, do some of your friends rush in to agree? These are not real friends. A real friend would say, 'Will you cut the blame crap and quit complaining about what they did to you? What did you do? What can you do to fix it?' That's what an honest friend will do for you."
—MILTON KATSELAS, director (*Butterflies Are Free*)

"In filming, the amounts of money involved are vast, so the natural tendency is to play the blame game. But what I have found is that the most successful people stop playing it, somewhere along the line. Correct yourself whenever you start a sentence with, 'I'm not blaming X, but. . . .' That is merely disguised and sterile self-justification. Instead, ask yourself, 'What did I not do right, or overlook doing?'

"Maybe you did nothing wrong, and included everything. But . . . maybe not. At least with self-examination, versus self-justification, you're taking control and responsibility, so you and the project can move ahead."
—DANIEL PETRIE, director (*A Raisin in the Sun*)

"Often, the individual you're blaming doesn't know you have a grievance. The agent may be unaware the client wants better access. The producer or whomever doesn't know the actor feels he deserves a better salary or conditions. Don't be afraid to ask! People aren't clairvoyant, and most are so busy that well more than details may fall between the cracks. You've a mouth; open it. Don't just use it for a cake hole." —JOHN INMAN, British actor (*Are You Being Served?*)

"If you have a legitimate beef regarding a casting director or a director or anybody, have your agent deal with it. It's the accepted method, sort of a good-cop, bad-cop scenario. You don't want to come off as the bad guy, if you can help it." —STARK HESSELTINE, agent

"In life, you never lie to your doctor or your lawyer. In Hollywood, you don't lie to your agent. He does that for you." —KIRK DOUGLAS

"I once got booked into a nightmare gig by a manager, who told me about it the day before. My agent, who's maybe a more convincing actor than I am, got me out of it." —TROY DONAHUE (*A Summer Place*)

"Agents get ten percent of an actor's income. Managers get whatever the talent's willing to part with. Elvis Presley handed over half his money to the so-called Colonel, who didn't have his best interests at heart.

'Tom Parker,' as he called himself, was in it for the dough, period.

"Elvis wanted to, but he never got to, do concerts overseas. Even after he faded in the U.S., Europe and Japan and Australia, etc., still wanted him in the flesh. Never mind that there was more and more of it. But Parker said no . . . see, the guy was an illegal alien. If he'd have accompanied Elvis abroad, he wouldn't have been allowed back into the U.S. Parker had no passport. . . . If there's a moral to this, it's to really, closely check out your manager." —OTIS BLACK-WELL, songwriter (Presley's "Don't Be Cruel")

"The first rule of thumb in my profession is to never, never, never perform for high society. They will murder you; they will destroy your will to live through their toxic inattention." —RITA MORENO, on performing at the Royal Room in Palm Beach, Florida

"I love performing live, but honey, I draw the line. Some audiences are too difficult to please and some venues aren't worth it. I like money, but earning it should be rewarding in either sense of the word!" —ANN MILLER (*Kiss Me, Kate*)

"As you get older, you fortunately grow less desperate. You won't do any old thing for the money, and if a proposition sounds ridiculous, it probably will be." —MADELYN PUGH, cowriter of *I Love Lucy*

"Young actors usually don't believe that there comes a time when it's hard to say no to a job offer just because it is a job offer. By then, it's not about needing the dough, it's about wanting to keep busy. But you want to keep busy at a certain level of quality—which you don't have to worry about when you're beginning, so long as you avoid doing porno."
—CRAIG STEVENS, TV's "Peter Gunn"

"I always have the fear that my last job may be my last job . . . I feel relieved or even grateful by the time the next offer comes along." —HENRY FONDA

"I believe an artist dies twice. The first time it's just terrible; I've been there when the phone isn't ringing for years. But the most important thing is not to implode. People go from the mountain into the valley and click into that dark, reptilian part of their brain and self-destruct. I see it all the time." —SYLVESTER STALLONE

"It's like holding sand in your hands when you have projects in this business that just don't happen. 'I thought that we were going to be doing so-and-so in June.' Well, they didn't get the money or the script is not ready or the studio changed heads. . . . All kind of stuff shifts and it's constantly in flux. Hopefully you've always got a lot of projects ahead of you. Hopefully one or two of them will pan out." —MORGAN FREEMAN

"I've got a few scripts I'm reading, and they're all absolute rubbish. But if you wait for a good script, you might wait forever. You finally have to say, 'Well, how much money will I get for this one, Charley?' One has to live, you know, and live well." —CHRISTOPHER PLUMMER

"I was offered to take my lecture tour to Japan. But I'd already visited Sweden. The audience there was polite and tried to respond, but the language difference intruded, to our mutual frustration. How, then, to try and scale the insuperable barrier of performing in English for the Japanese? I said no." —QUENTIN CRISP, author-actor-raconteur (*Orlando*)

"For sure, learn to wait . . . hesitate. Don't ever be too quick to say yes." —KIM BASINGER, who was sued for backing out of the sexist film *Boxing Helena*, about a woman voluntarily left armless and legless by a man

"I shocked the hell out of my agent when I turned down an offer to do a cigarette ad for $50,000. Other people were doing it at the time, but I knew I didn't want to have to create an excuse to myself, to her, and to others, for making money so that people could get cancer." —ALAN ALDA

"I like movies, certain movies—it depends. But I love the theater. I didn't get into acting to be a 'star.' So

making the decision was easy. I stuck to my principles."
—TOVAH FELDSHUH, who quit a film and
$100,000 after learning it required nudity which she
hadn't agreed to

"The movie became a hit, to say the least. But I turned
that down because it offended me, and I've had no
regrets since." —DORIS DAY, on declining to play
Mrs. Robinson in *The Graduate*; Anne Bancroft took
the role

"I'm known for, I guess, doing a stretch. I didn't get
pushed out of shape when they offered me [the part
of George Rockwell, head of the American Nazi
party, in *Roots II*]. I would have been upset if anyone
thought I shared any of their so-called values."
—MARLON BRANDO

"Stars, any people with clout, need to put their foot
down and do what's decent. It's always dishearten-
ing when an actor or actress known for being lib-
eral uses a needless antigay slur on screen. A hero
or star should not be seen to condone bigotry."
—Sir IAN MCKELLEN, openly gay actor (*The Hobbit* series)

"I shouldn't have said that [homophobic] word. It was
uncalled for, hurtful, and irrelevant to the scene. Today
it's much less acceptable . . . I heard it was cut from the
video or DVD version. But that doesn't happen with

most movies. They leave everything in." —MARY STEENBURGEN (*Time After Time*)

"Possibly the only thing I won't do in a picture is cross-dress. That's too frequently used for a stereotype and as a putdown of the homophile community. In my considerable experience, most 'gay' men are quite indifferent to women's apparel." —Sir JOHN GIELGUD

"I go by my instincts. If it's something I don't want to do, I don't. If it feels uncomfortable, I decline." —BARBRA STREISAND

"Maybe I didn't say no often enough when I was younger. You name it, I've broken it. I'm more careful now. But how careful do I want to be?" —JACKIE CHAN, known for performing most of his own stunts

"There are guidelines for actors about not doing something that sounds dangerous, per the Screen Actors Guild. But when you're asked on the set, when they implore you and it's made to sound so simple and so important to the movie . . . it's not easy to say no. Depending on a director or producer, you can create anger and resentment by saying no. They can make it very difficult for you. Damn them." —GORDON SCOTT, a former Tarzan

"Special-effects people are all the same. They like

things that go 'boom,' and they always say, 'No, don't worry, everything's safe.' But there's always a risk. That's what I've learned. As an actor, you have to keep the special-effects people away from you a little bit. Because here's the truth: everybody screws up once in a while, and so do they. The difference is, not everybody is playing with explosives when they screw up, and you don't want to be there when it happens."
—RUTGER HAUER (*The Hitcher*)

"Don't let a tough-talking or a sweet-talking director push you into doing something you honestly believe you'll regret later." —MELISSA GILBERT, Screen Actors Guild president

"At the time, I didn't want to appear in pictures I wouldn't want my kids to see. I passed up some that became pretty popular. Then I'd wonder if I was being a little prudish, you know? But now, looking back, I'm glad I did what I did." —DICK VAN DYKE (*Mary Poppins*)

"You'll have to ask her if she regrets going topless. I don't think so, but women often put a smiling face over a feeling. . . . Of course it was my idea. But honestly I thought the scene, which got loads of publicity, would help the film, artistically and financially. It didn't help financially."
—BLAKE EDWARDS, who directed wife Julie Andrews in *S.O.B.*

"One reason Charlton Heston wasn't a very interesting actor is that his m.o. was displaying his admittedly statuesque self. More than interacting. He treated other actors more like props than onscreen intimates or adversaries. But it's what happens between characters that signifies, that interests and holds a spectator."—ED LIMATO, agent

"I once worked on Broadway in a musical of the famous Ethel Merman. I was shocked in rehearsals when she said her lines to the seats in the audience, not to me. I asked if that was how she was going to act when the seats were full. With an angry face she told me that was the way she had been doing it for many, many years, and that she would continue to do it just like that.

"I said, 'That does not mean you are right, it just means you are old.'" —FERNANDO LAMAS, Argentine heartthrob

"One thing I like better about camera acting is that with stage acting it's possible for your partner to play more to the audience than to you. Most directors and editors won't let that happen on film, even if the actor—or star—is so inclined." —MICHAEL SARRAZIN (*For Pete's Sake*)

"Some of us tend to be control freaks, and an aspect I thoroughly enjoy about directing a film is that I get to decide where the audience looks. With a play, a director has no control over what people in the audience choose to telescope in on." —JODIE FOSTER, actor-director

"Some directors have either a perverse sense of humor or a method that works for themselves alone. Like Otto Preminger, who often made actors tense. Sometimes he'd sneak up behind you while you were preparing for a take and scream, 'Relax!'" —TOM TRYON, actor (*The Longest Day*) turned novelist

"Artist or not, meditation helps unlock creativity. For actors, it helps corral your thoughts and discipline your mind. So often, your mind is elsewhere . . . meditation trains you to return your mind's focus to 'here.' To the 'now,' the present moment, to the current feeling. It opens you up emotionally and relaxes you." —DENNIS WEAVER

"Transcendental Meditation can be life-changing on several levels. One thing it does is develop good posture, which makes you feel better physically and about yourself. With time, good posture becomes an attitude of mind as well as body. . . . TM puts me in a good mood, ready to work at my peak." —MARY TYLER MOORE

"My back got slowly stronger and gave fewer problems. I had formerly spent a few days each year with a pulled back muscle, lying on the floor and waiting slowly to be better. That mysteriously stopped, seemingly for good." —PETER CONRADI, actor and author (*Going Buddhist*) on meditation

"For females and for secure males, some of the best posture training is ballet lessons. Posture separates leads and authority figures from actors more likely to be hired for sidekick or even loser roles. Do not underestimate the importance of posture—not in acting, nor in public.

"Bad posture identifies a victim or victim mentality. Good posture indicates confidence and self-esteem. Have you ever seen a sex symbol with bad posture?" —BRET ADAMS, agent

"When I prepare to do a serious role, I straighten my back, clear my throat, and try to think of a joke or a risible image. For contrast, you understand. I let my mood float . . . the last thing you want with a somber character is too much heaviness." —Sir JOHN GIELGUD

"I act a lot better if I've had a good laugh prior to the director's yelling, 'Action!' And it makes no difference if it's a light, amusing scene or a dark, tragic scene . . . I'm free and loose and available . . . totally open to be affected by one thing—what the other actor is doing or saying." —PETER FALK

"Men: learn how to smile—more, and sincerely. Not

by looking in the mirror, but *feeling*—on your face and, particularly, inside you. A winning smile comes from genuine feeling and is a big asset to any actor, even one playing a villain. Though more particularly for a male lead. Most actresses already have this." —NINA FOCH, actor-coach (*Spartacus*)

"I'd like to tell actors who are at the commencement of their career to please not be so serious. A few smiles on a set do help the day move faster. But so many younger actors are either dead serious or so secretly terrified that from the look of them you'd think they'd stepped into a morgue. Lighten up, kids!" —ROSS HUNTER, producer (*Imitation of Life*)

"In my first scene in any movie ever, Sean Penn dragged me out to a swamp, threw me down in the mud, raped and killed me and my girlfriend. We did the scene, we took a shower, put on new clothes, and did the scene again. All night long. That was my big break." —PETER SARSGAARD (*Dead Man Walking*)

"The material may seem inane, even ludicrous, but no matter the situation or the lines, you, the actor, must infuse it with believability. You must never be embarrassed by it, or it will show. If you can't act natural and unembarrassed, you don't belong in acting." —RUSSELL JOHNSON, Professor on *Gilligan's Island*

"Remember, your real 'instrument' is the other actor. And since you're acting together, it's easier to share your suspension of disbelief and to make believe— like kids do, together or individually." —MARION DOUGHERTY, casting director

"Our childhood memories about it may be blocked or forgotten, but we've all been told at some point to stop pretending and imagining, to grow up and face up to reality. Reality's all right, but for an actor imagination is absolutely crucial, so sometimes you have to work backwards." —DANIEL DAY-LEWIS (*Lincoln*)

"If you remember your parents and teachers and all their injunctions against making believe or imaginary friends, you have to overcome that for acting's sake. Actors must be in touch with their inner child. Anyone who's too adult isn't prone to act well." —FRED GWYNNE (*The Munsters*)

"I encourage and look for the inner child. However, I don't care to meet the inner brat." —PEGGY FEURY, acting coach

"Emotions are most easily expressed and released when the breath is high in the body. . . . See how a child's chest moves with its emotions." —CATHY HAASE, actor-author (*Acting for Film*)

"At the beginning of life, we're childish or childlike. Toward the end of life, we can be childlike. Through the whole middle of life we can be childlike if we're actors. I love that freedom." —DEMI MOORE

"My mother had a tough time of it, but she loved acting. It was an escape for her—that and the bottle. She coached actors. . . . My production company, Pennebaker, is her maiden name." —MARLON BRANDO

"My mother came from Belarus, married a cruel husband, and had seven children. Her last wish was to not be buried next to Pa. How she must have suffered." —KIRK DOUGLAS, who gave his production company his mother's first name, Bryna

"Susan was my given first name. My father's last name was Williams. My mother's was Stockard, which I like a lot. Channing is from the first husband. Anyway." —STOCKARD CHANNING (*The Men's Club*)

"Hispanic cultures honor both parents by using both their last names. . . . We only use one here, so I took my mother's, modifying the spelling." —SHIRLEY MACLAINE

"Some uninformed people are saying Rita Hayworth 'passed for white' because of her name change and dyeing her hair red. Rita was white—her father, from Spain, was Eduardo Cansino; her mother, from

Ireland, was Volga Haworth [sic]. The mother, like so many back then, let the father give their child all three of her original names: Margarita Carmen Cansino, reflecting only his background." —NEDRA VOLZ (*The Dukes of Hazzard*)

"I so admired Bette Davis because she could switch from a 'good' character to a 'bad' one and be convincing as either. I never felt I could play, even as I got older, somebody 'bad,' a villain. That was my loss, because as actresses get older, their roles get less sympathetic. It's best to cultivate both sides of the acting repertoire." —RITA HAYWORTH

"Loud voices, threats, and leering are what some actors think of when it comes to villain parts. No! One of the most convincing villains ever was Robert Ryan—watch him in any of his myriad films . . . what he achieves by stillness. A threatening stillness. And in *The Devil Wears Prada*, Meryl Streep is the boss from hell. Does she once raise her voice? No. It's not what you do; it's how you do it." —ED LIMATO, agent

"If you lower your voice—speaking softer, not deeper—the listener and the spectator will tend to move in closer to you. They'll pay closer attention. That works for the camera, thanks to the sound people. For the theater, however, you have to be heard by everyone who's paid for a ticket." —MARTIN SHAW, U.K. actor who played an American in *The Hound of the Baskervilles*

"In theater, stillness works like a close-up does on screen." —RON MARASCO, acting instructor and author (*Notes to an Actor*)

"I became more effective when I stopped using my hands so much. They took away attention from the words and made my characters more easy to ignore. For someone from a Latin culture, taming the hands takes an initial effort!" —ELIZABETH PEÑA (*Down and Out in Beverly Hills*)

"For *Funny Girl* [on Broadway], Barbra Streisand wasn't as authentic as the older Fanny Brice. She was so young, and her gestures were so big. Finally, I convinced her to dedicate an entire performance to her late father, whom she idolized. She did, and that did it. That night, she was mature, glowing, and believable. As well, she could replicate that performance by using the same emotional aid." —ALAN MILLER, coach-author (*A Passion for Acting*)

"Anyone can have a breakthrough performance that's wonderful. Once in a blue moon the stars align or inspiration hits, and suddenly, magic. The trick is repeating it. And repeating it again. And again . . . which is where technique and training and craft come in. And those do take time. What do you expect? Overnight?" —GLORIA STUART (*Titanic*)

"I heard a director say, 'I need a butcher in this part.'

Someone suggested he get a real butcher who knew how to cut up meat. The director answered, 'If I've got a good actor, I've got a real butcher. If I've got a real butcher, the minute I put him in front of the camera, he's stiff and I've got a bad actor.'" —MICHAEL CAINE

"It's all in the mind, acting is. I was directing Julie Christie in *Far From the Madding Crowd*. During a break an actor was telling Julie how stiff his costume was. She said the secret of a period picture is that one's costume should feel like clothes, not a costume. If the clothing was stiff, those were stiffer, more rigid times. In point of fact, that actor's character was supposed to be stiff and priggish.

"You must inhabit your character's costumes until they become your character's clothes and, eventually, *your* clothes." —JOHN SCHLESINGER

"Don't think of the character you're playing as 'she,' but 'me.'" —JENNIFER ANISTON

"Don't think of the size or prestige or relative economics of the movie you're in. Each movie is its own world; and the characters in it, that is their world and it's very important to them. Just don't compare to other projects, other actors. Do what you have to do, with all you have." —RYAN GOSLING (*The Ides of March*)

"I remember when I was 26. I was doing an interview and this guy said, 'Don't you feel that lesser actors are passing you by? Are you avoiding success; are you afraid of success?' And I thought, 'My God, I've just worked with John Sayles, Woody Allen, and Stephen Frears!' He wanted to know why I wasn't Tom Cruise. . . . This journalist was a smart guy writing for a good magazine, but he was so indoctrinated. I thought I was winning, ya know? . . . Tom Cruise wants to produce *Mission: Impossible 2* and *3*. That's his deal, what he gets off on." —JOHN CUSACK

"Show me a bad script, and I will show you a big payday. Conversely, show me a really great script, and forget it. You're lucky if you don't have to pay for it." —AL PACINO

"I've had better experiences making smaller movies than bigger studio films. Factor out the layer of executives, and then you can concentrate on what really matters." —MANDY MOORE (*Because I Said So*)

"When you're shooting something and you're all in makeup and costume and an executive or a group of suits walks in, even if they stay quiet and in the background, it's unnerving. Like when the principal walks into your classroom . . . something vaguely threatening. But you learn to put them out of your mind, to stay in character, and keep relating to your other characters.

"A good rule of thumb: ignore the suits; have as little to do with them as possible." —KEVIN BACON

"The money men necessary for making movies, or the TV sponsors and executives, can be depressing. They're so bottom-line, often so grim and critical. Probably just jealous they're not creative, and *so* replaceable." —WINONA RYDER

"Movies are terrifically optimistic enterprises. If you come into the makeup trailer in the morning and you say to the hair person, 'Did you go to the dailies?' I've never in my life heard anybody say, 'They weren't very good.' It's always, 'Oh, my God! It's electrifying!'" —CHRISTOPHER WALKEN

"There are people in the business who try to be kind and not let you down. They don't like to say no. But it gets awfully frustrating that they almost never say yes." —BETTY GARRETT (*Laverne and Shirley*)

"I was trying different agents, trying to figure out different ways to push myself. People just weren't interested. You knew the career was dead as soon as you showed up on both *Love Boat* and *Murder, She Wrote*." —JACKIE EARLE HALEY, ex–teen star who seldom worked over the next three decades until a 2007 Academy Award nomination

"The thing to do if you're a regular on TV is to get into

at least one feature film during each hiatus. 'Cause if they can't associate a hit movie or two with your name, you'll be stuck in TV-land, and that's an exceedingly hard place to break out of." —FREDDIE FIELDS, agent

"I was in movies before TV. . . . After my series (*Bewitched*), I could have fought to get back into the movies. But human-interest films about people, not killer robots and special effects, were no longer being made as studio movies—they were now made-for-TV movies. So I'm doing good, grown-up, character-driven TV movies. . . . No one would make a Hollywood movie about Lizzie Borden anymore, but I got to play her on television, which more people see anyway.

"Didn't Bette Davis say that the best special effect is talent? I agree! Talent, plus a good story."
—ELIZABETH MONTGOMERY

"There's a fine line between doing something because you believe it's the right thing to do, and guessing what the public wants. . . . You have to be quite vigilant with yourself and question why you're doing certain things, as well as what's behind all that. Otherwise, you can find yourself having made choices for the wrong reasons, and suddenly you're a completely different person than the one you thought you were a year ago." —MICHAEL SHEEN (*Midnight in Paris*)

"I freely admit it: I sold out. Nowadays I only take a role for money. I have no interest in acting. I got disgusted with Hollywood, the blacklist, the backstabbing, the posturing, all of it, years ago." —STERLING HAYDEN (*The Long Goodbye*)

"I have worked all over the world, and I find it's not so much where you work but what you're working on. Good work is possible anywhere, at any budget. The same with bad work." —JEANNE MOREAU, French star

"Never stop working on yourself. As an actor and as a human being." —UTA HAGEN, actor-coach

"You can become a better actor by becoming a more complete human being, and you can become a more complete human being by becoming a better actor." —TED DANSON (*Cheers*)

"Wanting to be a star is about wanting money and needing adulation. Well-adjusted individuals want to excel at their job. I'm an actor. I want to be a very good actor." —JOHNNY DEPP

"I am an actress, not a star." —BETTE DAVIS, star actor

"Stardust is what we are all made of, if the Big Bang Theory is correct. So far, it is the most correct explanation. The stars, even our sun, shine upon us with indifference . . . it is up to us to make sense and value of our lives on this smaller planet." —Dr. HAING S. NGOR (*Heaven and Earth*)

"Theater people used to look down on the movies, and then came television, so movie people had something to look down on. Now, what is there to look down on? Or, more importantly, what is there to look up at?" —MADELINE KAHN (*What's Up, Doc?*)

"Film is sometimes art. An art of manipulating time and space. Artifice . . . artificial, yet very real to spectators—all the more so if the actors speak and move convincingly." —JAMES IVORY, director, of Merchant Ivory

"Film acting is harder for me than stage work . . . I'm much more of an endurance athlete than I am a sprinter, and movies are all about the sprint. I love the marathon aspect of a play." —JAKE GYLLENHAAL

"Stage acting is harder in that you have to memorize your entire role, not just a scene or a few lines. But camera and sound requirements make screen acting tough. For some actors, hitting their marks is easy. Others have to practice at home, with pieces of masking tape on the floor or small objects on the carpet.

"Then there's learning and remembering that if your character is excited or for some reason speaking faster, you're not supposed to go louder—unless the script calls for it—but you have to maintain your intensity. And when you're talking low, you have to maintain the energy. And so on!" —KARL MALDEN, Oscar winner

"Did you know you have to slow down certain movements for the camera? Otherwise they look jerky. However, as you slow down a given move, you mustn't slow down your speech. It's not as facile as people imagine." —KEIRA KNIGHTLEY

"There is such a thing as a 'television rise,' when, to get out of a chair, instead of doing it normally—the natural thing is to lower your head as you start to get up— you put one leg under the chair and use it to smoothly glide up and out of the chair. This allows a camera that is on your face to follow you easily as you get up." —PATRICK TUCKER, U.K. director-coach

"Whatever the medium of acting, I think its nonfinancial joy and usefulness lies in getting it off your chest. By expressing emotions—whoever's— actors don't grow emotionally stale and locked in, like so many people who don't have an outlet. I think it also keeps actors younger than most people." —DEL ARMSTRONG, makeup artist to Rita Hayworth, Lana Turner, et al.

"Film acting, TV acting, stage acting, acting in life, they're all about persuasion . . . about being allowed to fulfill a desire, about moving toward achieving a goal. Hopefully a worthwhile one." —MARTIN RITT, director (*Norma Rae*)

"An actor's goal is not to be interesting. That is a script's goal. Yours is to be truthful." —GLENN CLOSE

5

COPING

"Coping in show business has everything to do with resiliency. Can you bounce back? Do you bounce back on your own? It has to come from within. You have to learn to hold your own hand." —AUDREY MEADOWS (*The Honeymooners*)

"It's simple. When I think I can't cope with the big-time pressures, I pause to think back to when I was, you know, aspiring . . . struggling and hoping. Hoping for the situation and even the problems I have now." —JACK NICHOLSON

"When I was [growing up] in Missouri, I wished on and sort of idealized Hollywood. Now I sometimes idealize and wish for Missouri. But that's about the grass being greener, isn't it? You've got to deal with what you have and where you're at." —BRAD PITT

"Nostalgia isn't what it used to be." —SIMONE SIGNORET, Oscar-winning French actress

"Don't dwell on the past. Let others bring it up. If your glory years were long ago, who wants to be reminded how long ago that was? But at least you had them, and no one can take them away from you." —JAY R. SMITH, ex–child actor who played Pinky in the *Our Gang* movie series

"For the newcomer to acting, the best is yet to come. For some of us who scored major success early, then experienced an inevitable downslide, we hope the worst is behind us. I don't look back if I can help it." —JOHN TRAVOLTA

"Since in no way can you influence the past, what's the use of focusing on it? A little reminiscence goes a long way, baby." —TELLY SAVALAS

"Anticipation provides half the fun in life. One should never be so successful or so old that one doesn't look forward—in both senses of that phrase." —IRVING RAPPER (*Now, Voyager*), director who lived to 101

"American actors and especially American actresses are so fearful of age. But every being that still breathes is aging. If you're not aging, you are dead. So be happy!" —PENELOPE CRUZ

"As the Chinese say, 'Do not resist aging—many never

get the chance.' It's particularly true for actors. Look how many died in middle age. Or never reached it."
—NANCY KWAN (*The World of Suzie Wong*)

"The older I get, the wider the range of roles I can fill, and the more emotions I can realistically tap . . . I'm not the same in everything I do, but I bring myself to everything I do." —LINDA LAVIN, star of stage and TV (*Sean Saves the World*)

"One advantage of stage versus camera is that if you think and behave on stage as if you're handsome or beautiful, the audience will think you are. True. Dame Edith Evans had a slightly froglike face but won acclaim playing a beauty in a famous play." —Sir ALEC MCCOWEN (*Travels with My Aunt*)

"Dolores del Rio, the Mexican movie star, was still beautiful in her seventies when she was touring. I once saw her in the wings just before she went on stage—her arms were raised and she was fluttering her fingers and hands. . . . They explained she was self-conscious about some veins on the back of her hands. The hand-fluttering was to energize her and to temporarily make the veins disappear. I never noticed them anyway." —RICARDO MONTALBAN (*Fantasy Island*)

"Don't dream on the past, don't obsess about the future. Just occupy yourself in the present. That'll make for a better future." —JEFF COREY, blacklisted actor and, later, acting coach

"There are those who say the struggle to achieve success is the fun part, not the success itself. I doubt that those who say such a thing achieved much success, or they wouldn't be saying it. Besides, doesn't it depend on how hard and long the struggle is? I *mean.* . . ." —MARY WOLF HUNTER, Broadway director (*Peter Pan*)

"When you're up and coming, reviews can mean too much to you. The bad ones can be devastating . . . I remember the name of every critic that gave me a bad review. I keep a list—and believe me, I won't be doing any of those people any favors. . . ." —JENNIFER LOPEZ

"No matter how outstanding a performance and how acclaimed by the public, there will always be some critics to carp and disagree. An actor's life becomes emotionally easier if you avoid reading reviews . . . I love the story that some Frenchman, I think, told about phoning or writing to a critic who'd given him an awful review. He said, 'I am sitting in the smallest room of my house. Your review is before me. Soon it will be behind me.'" —GRAHAM CHAPMAN (*The Life of Brian*)

"Advice to actresses of stage and screen: do not read

reviews by John Simon if you appear on stage or screen. He criticizes an actress's looks, he is hurtful, and he seems to relish building a negative reputation from misogyny, sexism, and other forms of bigotry. If you doubt this, read some of his reviews of *other* actresses." —RADIE HARRIS, columnist

"Notices are for audiences and insecure actors. Your audience will tell you if you're good. Your technique assures you that you're good. The length of your [stage] run tells you if your vehicle is good." —Dame JUDITH ANDERSON (*Medea*)

"Bear in mind that reviews aren't written to help actors. Ever." —JONATHAN HARRIS, Dr. Smith on TV's *Lost in Space*

"Part of surviving and coping as a performer is knowing what to expect. Show business isn't fantasyland or wonderland. It's a very bottom-line business, and you are the product. Get used to thinking of yourself as a product. Like Vitameatavegamin!" —JUDY TENUTA, comedian-actor

"Soon after I became famous, I saw how reporters treat[ed] me like something instead of someone. Like an aphrodisiac. . . . They didn't want my opinions and thoughts. So why waste my time in interviews? They only want to see how I look. . . . So, to keep them away, sometimes I say things to shock. In

1959, I announce[d] that *haute couture* is only for grandmothers. It shocks the nation, and for years most of them leave me alone, ha-ha." —BRIGITTE BARDOT, French icon

"I went to an audition, which, when it concluded, the casting director said, 'So now you want to act. . . .' I stared, then said, 'I've been acting for some time.' He said, 'So you gave up writing some time ago?' I said, 'I don't write.' To cut to the chase, he thought I was Patrick Dennis, the author of *Auntie Mame*. I politely asserted, 'No, I'm Dennis Patrick, the actor.'

"The c.d. smiled at me and said, I swear, 'I apologize. I guess I was just in the wrong aisle of the supermarket.' Nonetheless, and pardon the expression, I did book the job!" —DENNIS PATRICK (*Dallas*)

"A movie-star friend once told me he deliberately tries to sound boring in interviews so they won't seek him out so often. Good tactic! I don't have to worry—I do sound boring in interviews." —JAMES GARNER

"When your new movie comes out, the studio puts you in a hotel suite and you sit there, while one by one each interviewer comes in. It's almost like being a hooker . . . you try to think of something new to say and to act like you haven't heard the same question 19 times before, that same day." —JANE FONDA

"If you've ever taken a commercials-acting class, you

know the #1 criterion for getting an ad is product enthusiasm. You act it, of course. . . . Actors are usually contractually obligated to publicize a film. If your film isn't very special, it can get boring promoting it in interviews. Again, you act. I pretend it's a product—which it is—and I enthuse about the movie, my role in it, my costars, the crew, anything I can think of. I do my job!" —JILL CLAYBURGH (*An Unmarried Woman*)

"One of the perks of not being a leading man, although I have starred in a handful of choice pictures, is carrying a lighter burden. I don't have to pose for as many photographs, I'm not asked to do product endorsements, I'm not called upon to publicize the latest picture I appear in—inasmuch as I'm usually the villain—and I don't have to act cheerful or pretend the leading lady was a sweetheart when perhaps she was a swine." —GEORGE SANDERS, winner of a Best Supporting Actor Oscar

"Any public figure worth their salt is into enthusiasm. Actor or politician, you try to move people, to involve them. Enthusiasm is crucial for an actor and for her audience! It's a do-it-yourself thing, but it does help you—in the short run and the long run." —JACQUELINE BISSET

"Enthusiasm in public and in publicity keeps you

fresh and interesting. If you don't think you're up to it, go back to acting class. If you think it's beneath you, come back to planet Earth." —COLIN FARRELL

"Robert Mitchum was able to get away with that sleepy-eyed, don't-give-a-damn look and manner. People found it sexy or intriguing. But don't ignore the double standard. What actress could get away with that? People would think she's aloof, bored, arrogant, unappreciative; why put up with her? Be careful whom you copy, should you feel the ignoble need to copy." —SUSANNAH YORK

"Don't assume you are unique. Even if a role's breakdown description is very specific, you'll still find 50 other actors there to try out for it. Concentrate more on what's inside you than on how you look, because looks-wise, actors are less unique than ever. I call it The Clone Syndrome." —JAMES CRABE, cinematographer (*The Formula*)

"I had one acting instructor who missed his calling as a drill sergeant. In fact, he'd played several small military roles. He made it a big point that you should never assume anything, not in your working life, nor in your private life. The very first class, he wrote out ASSUME in block letters on the blackboard and barked at us, 'When you "assume," you make an *ass* out of *u* and *me*!'" —ANNE BANCROFT

"You can develop personality, talent, charm, spontaneity, and more. But your looks can only be developed so far, and even less for a male actor." —BENEDICT CUMBERBATCH (*Star Trek Into Darkness*)

"For a long time, I was self-conscious about my upper front teeth. When I smiled and saw it on camera I couldn't ignore that I had major teeth. So I tried not to smile, but that only developed a set of problems. . . . An acting coach confided that she loved my smile, that it was my 'badge of sincerity.' She iterated how special I was, and not to be concerned with being different, just act natural. She helped put me more at ease, and I resumed smiling freely." —SANDY DENNIS, Tony and Oscar winner

"I've heard time and again that actors should 'act natural.' The correct phrasing is 'be natural.' There is a chasm of difference." —JOCELYN BRANDO, actress and Marlon's sister

"Not every actor has a distinctive personality. Some male stars are basically a look or type, more than a personality or talent. But they fit handily into action projects and Westerns—they play cardboard heroes. They simply fill a slot. . . . Actors ought to worry less about 'talent' than believability. Just be believable saying your lines. That's enough for a start. For

some stars, it's enough for a start and a long career."
—MARION DOUGHERTY, casting director

"One quote from an interview I gave has become sort of famous. From when I said I didn't think I had a personality. Like, compared to my father [actor Vic Morrow, killed on the set of *The Twilight Zone*], who did have one. But you know, time changes things and it heals and it creates things . . . I have a personality now."
—JENNIFER JASON LEIGH

"Figuring out if you're more suited to comedy or drama isn't always easy. But it usually turns out you don't have to. Others will do it for you. Some industry people—like, some actors' managers—would decide and change everything about you if they could, including your name and hair color. It's that Pygmalion thing of wanting to create someone from scratch. You at least want to hold on to your personal essence."
—LINDSAY LOHAN

"If you feel limited by drama, seek out comedy. You can look and act wildly and diversely in comedy, and you don't have to do it alone. Create a duo or a troupe. Test the waters in clubs and live venues. Then try the telly. Finally, if you're viable enough, make it in the movies! I did, leading man and all." —GRAHAM CHAPMAN (*Monty Python's Flying Circus*)

"A lot of people that start out as actors transition

to other fields. Everything from casting directors to talk-show hosts and movie directors, TV execs, politicians—no comment!—agents, writers, etc. I guess because most felt they were powerless or stagnant as actors. That whole thing of Hitchcock saying actors are cattle—replaceable and manipulated." —SAM JAFFE, agent-producer (*Born Free*)

"Every profession has its problems. But no matter their level of success, actors worry more than most employees and are more dependent than most—on their looks, age, and image; on producers, studios, and networks; on the public. For a smooth or steady ride, pick anything but acting!" —T. R. KNIGHT (*Grey's Anatomy*)

"Don't go into acting to become happy or to escape from yourself. You can't do the latter, and the former has to come from within, whatever your career is." —BORIS KARLOFF

"People who are unhappy being stars were unhappy *before* they were stars." —JESSICA SIMPSON

"I think most of the hardness or pretentiousness I have seen in actors is from being hurt. I think it is their defense. They would rather be first to hurt someone else." —Dr. HAING S. NGOR, Oscar winner

"Partly I got into show business to become rich

and famous and thus show up anyone who'd treated me badly growing up. But doesn't one evolve with maturity? My focus ultimately changed from negative to positive, as I found that I enjoyed the work, even the struggle, for its own sake."
—MICHAEL LANDON

"I wasn't crazy about my original last name, so I changed it. As most actors did, or had to. One relative reminded me that I'd always wanted to 'show them' and asked me how 'they' would know it was me if they didn't recognize my name? I hesitated to answer her. Until, about the time I turned 30, I realized, and told her, that you can't live your life *against*, you have to live it *for*." —DIANA DORS, *née* Fluck, blonde British bombshell

"Living well is the best revenge, but it helps if other people know you're doing it." —MICHAEL CAINE

"A lot of people want to be me. But they just want to be me now. They don't want, and couldn't want, to be the me who had to go through so much crap to get to where I'm at now." —HENRY ROLLINS, actor-musician

"Everyone thinks once you become a celebrity, you change a lot. That's not so. *They* change—toward *you*. The relationship changes. It changes, or it just stops."
—MEG RYAN

"People are more comfortable with their peers. That's why most stars hobnob with other stars, and just plain folks party with just plain folks. Birds of a feather. . . ."
—JANE FONDA

"Your bosom buddy from high school or college who doesn't become a successful actor will almost invariably be either intimidated by you or jealous of you. It's tough keeping your friends from the real world."
—JIM CARREY

"Once you become a hit in the acting arena, it seems everyone's ready to take a potshot. Suddenly, everyone's a critic. And too much of it's not constructive criticism." —DANNY DEVITO

"Now, if I'm in a supermarket and accidentally knock something over, everyone looks and feels free to speculate. It can make news, and someone might even for spite lie and say I was drunk or throwing a tantrum."
—SHARON STONE

"My relatives don't know how to handle my fame . . . 'I need a new roof for my house.' They assume I'm rich. They'll say things like that because they don't know what else to say. I don't even go to family reunions anymore."—JAMES EARL JONES

"Celebrated actors earn a lot of money. Not all of them stay wealthy. But I'll tell you this: the poor actors also get it right and left from people wanting to overcharge them—everyone from the florist to the plumber to the auto mechanic and the caterer, the gardener, even the pizza delivery." —JAKE GORDON, Hollywood business manager

"Everything in life has its price. Being rich does, and being famous does. It can be quite wonderful, overall. But great success closes a lot of doors, among them those to privacy, not worrying about your image, being liked for yourself, not having to be concerned with wacko fans, trusting people freely, aging gracefully . . . need I continue?" —HUGH GRANT

"Once you're an actor on camera, a large chunk of you belongs to the public. Like it or not. That's the cost of fame. You are no longer a private citizen, staring is allowed, and to some irreversible degree you are now a product." —JACK LEMMON

"I always heard criticism is the tax on fame. They were right. And then some." —BRAD PITT

"Before success, an actor's life can be difficult. It's even more difficult once you achieve success—in other words, maintaining your success. . . ." —JACK L. WARNER, mogul

"Enjoy the ride, because you may or may not reach your intended destination. And it may be a very different place than you imagined." —KIM BASINGER, Oscar winner

"I thought if I became a successful actress, it would give me the world. Instead, everyone wants me to give to them, and now I am not sure if they like me really or for what they think I can give them." —KATINA PAXINOU, Oscar winner (*For Whom the Bell Tolls*)

"I came from a poor part of Spain and went into show business so I could afford to eat. But after I became famous, I found out I cannot afford to eat—I am always dieting, to keep my figure." —CHARO, ageless sex symbol and classical guitarist

"This business is tough on men, but it's shit on women." —DIANE LADD

"Being a celebrity can cause an accidental cheapening of the things one holds dear. A slip of the tongue in an interview, and it's easy for me to feel I've sold out some private part of my life in exchange for publicity." —STEVE MARTIN

"Some people just expect too much. Like the movie-star actress everyone knows is [a] lesbian, but she's always asking for her privacy. Or the movie star with a wife who propositions every guy under 30, then gets upset when reporters mention the rumors." —ROSEANNE BARR, who has an openly lesbian sister and an openly gay brother

"Keeping a low profile has to do with not going to places where the paparazzi are. It's not that hard. A lot of celebrities moan about how difficult it is, then they keep showing up at film premieres. Why do you show up?" —JOHN CUSACK

"People who have car collections—I never understood that. I always thought that was unnecessary. It's not beautiful, it's not creative. It's just showing how much money you've got." —DANIEL RADCLIFFE, aka "Harry Potter"

"I've had people come up and ask me to sign their guns. Sign my name on gun handles and holsters and stuff. I've done it once or twice for law-enforcement officials, but when people do that, I always tell them no. I don't want my name on that, and I hope you use this gun wisely." —CLINT EASTWOOD

"The thing is not to be an actor, first, last and always. There's all the rest of life. There are people not in 'the industry.' There's the rest of the world—and notice that most actors, no matter how rich, seldom travel and see the world. Also, most actors don't read books, they read scripts.

"I don't admire the actor who becomes famous, buys a mansion, then puts up a high wall between himself and the world, thinking of nothing but his next project and his next salary. Pitiful." —JEREMY BRETT, TV's "Sherlock Holmes"

"With success you find, sooner or later, that you don't have to lift a finger to make enemies. I never did! They're counterproductive. But like barnacles, they accrue. My eventual solution was to ignore them, or if I couldn't and ran into them—I don't mean while driving, unfortunately—I just smile and act as nicely toward them as toward anyone else. That really throws them.

"People who choose to be enemies want to get a rise out of you. They feel cheated if they don't get it." —JOAN COLLINS

"If you hold a grudge, it makes more of an impression on you than the person it's against. Let it go. Let things go. Life's too short, and careers are even shorter." —BEN AFFLECK, actor-director-producer (*Argo*)

"There are two things you can do about enemies. Either let them get you down, making you feel depressed, taking up your time with negative thoughts, generating self-doubts, etc.

"Or, use them. As a spur. To make you work harder, to make you better than them, to make you happier than them. Because those people are secretly quite unhappy, secretly very small." —NIGEL HAWTHORNE (*The Madness of King George*)

"I would be lost without my enemies! They are the measure of my success; when they stop caring and spitting in my direction, I shall know I'm slipping. My enemies invigorate me." —MARIA CALLAS, opera diva

"Expect to have enemies, especially the longer you're in the business. But don't waste time or energy on them." —TONY RANDALL

"One of the biggest movie stars was a political witch hunter who in the 1950s secretly helped fund the Ku Klux Klan. Many still idolize him, but he made enemies galore. His alcoholism wasn't publicized, but he was a very angry man. A possible reason, according to several women who knew him privately, is that he was, let us say, undersized." —JOYCE HABER, *Los Angeles Times* columnist

"If a man is secure in himself and about himself, he may be a happy actor. However, generally speaking, actresses are happier than actors. Unless they're married to actors, who tend to make them unhappy." —JOAN BENNETT (*Dark Shadows*)

"Some actors torture themselves by taking their work too seriously. Stars, in particular, and males more than females. Actresses often have children, which may keep us more grounded. The work of childrearing puts outside work into perspective." —MAUREEN STAPLETON, Oscar winner

"Being glamorous can grow dull quickly. It takes a lot of work, for one thing. And you have to maintain that artificial, glamorous attitude. You can't be glamorous at home. Even less so when you're a mommy."
—TINA LOUISE (*Gilligan's Island*)

"If you're not a good actor, your kids will see right through you. Mine keep me on my professional toes!"
—RON HOWARD, actor turned director

"Athletes and actors are performers. Their work is public, so they can easily obsess over it. They need to get outside interests. I mean, if you were an accountant and that's all you talked about and all your friends were accountants, people would tell you to get a life. I should know, having been an accountant." —BOB NEWHART

"What you need to not do, as an actor, is take your work home with you, even if you live alone. Your own life is tough enough without inflicting your character's problems and conflicts onto your private time and space, let alone your family." —KEANU REEVES

"Most of an actor's life is spent looking for work, interviewing, auditioning, hoping for callbacks, seeking a better agent, networking, trying to submit yourself. The only steady employment is a long-running TV series, and after that it's usually downhill, because you've become stereotyped. So before you become an actor, really think about it. *Really* think. That red carpet they show so often on TV is for only about one in a hundred actors." —KATE NELLIGAN (*The Prince of Tides*)

"Besides some talent and a lot of persistence, every actor needs two things: hope and a sense of humor." —JENNIFER LAWRENCE, Oscar winner (*Silver Linings Playbook*)

"Buddhists say you need three things in life: something to do, something to love, and something to hope for. Isn't that great?" —DICK VAN DYKE

"If you love what you do, that is the first thing in life. And the last. Because mates will leave you or die, children will move out and away, but work—filling your time with effort and achievement—that always remains to you. I always knew I would end up alone and that I would work until the end." —BETTE DAVIS, who died while in Europe receiving yet another award

"I once heard Gore Vidal say he'd probably write until the bitter end. I would have thought he meant the happy end. If you're doing what you like, what's bitter? Unless it's one's personality. Bitter is doing what you don't like, am I right?" —JOANNE WOODWARD

"The best partner to accompany you through life is

your sense of humor. When the angst gets too heavy, just laugh—without thinking of something funny. Then think of something funny and laugh again. So much of life is a big joke, really. And without humor, it can be a big, big drag." —HEATHER GRAHAM

"Laugh with your friends, laugh at your enemies, and don't forget now and then to laugh at yourself." —WILL FERRELL

"There are also and often the little accomplishments. Daily things or occasional things. Feel good about them. Don't set aside joy for only big accomplishments, because those don't come along as often. Don't limit your happiness or inner smiles." —Dr. HAING S. NGOR, Oscar winner

"Don't let anyone belittle your goals or effort. No matter who it is, pull away. Nobody has that right. Or do those people not have any goals or make any effort? A friend or loved one supports your goals and effort. It's that simple." —BONNIE FRANKLIN (*One Day at a Time*)

"When someone discourages you and tries to push you in another direction, ignore their words of protest that they 'only want the best' for you. That is seldom true. Explore what they're really saying and what their motivation is. Discouragement should come only from your enemies." —HAL HOLBROOK

"In this business, there's always someone ready to dampen your spirit, no matter how high you go. When I won my Oscar, one reporter asked how I felt to be getting the award that should have been Jack Benny's. For once I was speechless. My dear friend Jack passed away before he could play the role, so I'd stepped in, and the Academy's voters apparently liked what I did, or I wouldn't have received the award. Of course, at the time it didn't occur to me to say that to the kindhearted reporter." —GEORGE BURNS, about *The Sunshine Boys*

"Success is what *you* make it out to be. I have known very successful coffin-makers and I've worked with unsuccessful Hollywood stars. . . . For myself, I decided success would mean owning my own golf course and my own bank. I made that happen. But those were *my* criteria. Everyone has or should have his own idea of success, and it shouldn't be anybody else's but his own." —SEAN CONNERY

"One of my husbands had a hobby of looking down on other people. It was so boring for me and it took so much of his time and energy. I left him when I realized that in spite of his money he was less of a success than most of the men he was criticizing." —LANA TURNER

"Success comes in big, small, and in-between sizes. As long as you consider what you do a success, it is. Look how many humongous stars were unhappy enough to try or succeed in killing themselves. So how successful were they, really?" —LISA KUDROW (*Friends*)

"It's wiser and more self-affirming for actors to measure success in terms of the pleasure of doing and the contentment afterward than in sheerly monetary terms." —PHIL HARTMAN (*Saturday Night Live*)

"It's quite feasible for a character actor to be more satisfied with his work and life than a leading man. I knew Tyrone Power well, and he was very conflicted, often frustrated and depressed. Not on screen, of course. Whilst I have played mostly villains—slimy, classy, and smug. As a real-life individual, I'm quite satisfied and rather smug." —GEORGE SANDERS (*All About Eve*)

"Naturally, who wouldn't want my father's career? But I wouldn't want the after part. The unemployment of a star or legend is not a happy thing." —SYDNEY CHAPLIN, actor and Charlie's son

"My father did things his way, often in defiance of custom. But he paid the price. But because he followed his own artistic vision and because he didn't pander to the noisy conservative bandwagon during the McCarthy era, he is now on a historic pedestal, and not just as an actor, writer, director, producer, and composer."—GERALDINE CHAPLIN (*Dr. Zhivago*)

"Critics kept saying we created the company for money. That was, no denying, one part of it. The more significant part, though, was obtaining creative freedom. And providing an example—showing that there could be an alternative to the hidebound established system." —CHARLIE CHAPLIN, who in 1919 cofounded United Artists with director D. W. Griffith, Mary Pickford, and Douglas Fairbanks

"The best way to get along in life or acting or anything is *your* way. Don't copy and don't listen. . . . I use so-called women's perfumes. Scent doesn't have a gender, but the manufacturers say 'perfume' instead of 'cologne' so they can sell it to women—dames with rich husbands—so the perfume brings in a lot higher price than the cologne. . . . My favorite scent is Vent Vert. It's a 'perfume' from Balmain, and it means *green wind*." —MARLON BRANDO

"I grew up in a household of don't-you-dare! I took refuge in libraries, where I learned about why-don't-you? That got my mind moving, and eventually moved me out. To New York and then to Hollywood." —VAN JOHNSON

"In Greece, my parents tried to fill me with much more shame than they would feed to a boy. 'Have you no shame?' That was supposed to create instant guilt and shame. But one day, at 15, when I heard that again, something inside me clicked. Suddenly I knew that being free of the feelings of shame that anybody else puts inside you is one of the requirements for being a well-adjusted human being." —IRENE PAPPAS (*Zorba the Greek*)

"It wasn't that difficult to stop being manipulated by your parents once you grew up and stopped needing their financial and practical support, was it? Alas and alack, it's considerably more difficult to avoid being emotionally manipulated by a director or producer, etc. These people who have hired you work their tricks on you in front of a small crowd." —JEFF COREY, actor-coach

"On the set and in my dressing room, the powers that be tried everything they could think of, short of outright threats—they did use intimidation and veiled threats—to get me to do a seminude scene I'd never agreed to do." —IRISH McCALLA (*Sheena, Queen of the Jungle*)

"I declined the nudity, but later they brought in a body double. The result was that everyone thought I did the nude scene anyway, and I had no grounds to sue, which anyhow you hardly dare to do if you want to keep on working." —CHERYL "RAINBEAUX" SMITH (*The Pom Pom Girls*)

"Mama meant well, it was the times. . . . She'd say she wanted her three daughters to grow up to be 'ladies,' like [actress] Irene Dunne. Of course now we know that 'lady' is less of a compliment than a restriction. Mama was one of relatively few actresses who campaigned openly for the Equal Rights Amendment. When it failed to pass, she couldn't believe it, and neither could I." —CARRIE HAMILTON, Carol Burnett's actor daughter

"I know a very struggling young actress who for whatever reasons of upbringing or inherent tendency is painfully self-conscious about being female, about her weight, her looks, her clothing. She can't say the word 'woman'—to her it's tainted and sexual. She doesn't say 'girl,' a female child, but she won't ever say 'woman.' So she calls every adult female a 'lady,' whether they are or not." —ROBERT DRIVAS (*The Illustrated Man*)

"Actors are imaginative. They have to be. Yet imagination can go too far. Where does personal fancy end and mental illness begin? Some actors hear voices. Among them one who played Joan of Arc! Others have intrusive thoughts—the basis of obsessive-compulsive disorder. What they fail to recognize is that unwanted or 'bad' thoughts are not actions. If it enters your head that you slap a loved one while they're nagging you, that doesn't mean you do it.

"We all have thoughts of every sort, some inappropriate. But they don't eventuate into action. We don't, or shouldn't, allow mere thoughts to get the

upper hand. However, I guess it's not that easy for a few people. Yet you know, some of these psychiatrically needy people do function as successful actors!"
—CHAIM POTOK, rabbi turned author whose novel *The Chosen* was made into a movie

"Don't devalue yourself because you're not white or male, Christian or heterosexual, or whatever else. Hollywood thrives on mass appeal, so women and minorities either get short shrift or they get stereotyped. If you're offered a stereotyped role, don't feel you have to accept it. If you do, feel free to make the suggestions to make it more realistic. Of course you catch more flies with honey than vinegar, honey."
—TED ROSS (*The Wiz*)

"You know, if you don't open your mouth, others will define you—incorrectly and adversely. That's why we had all these appalling gay movie stereotypes for so long. People stayed silent. That helped no one but our self-appointed enemies." —RON VAWTER (*Sex, Lies, and Videotape*)

"Believe it or not, if you are a Jewish actor at some point you will inevitably be discriminated against in Hollywood—by fellow Jews. If you're a gay actor, you'll inevitably be discriminated against in Hollywood by fellow gays. This is a sadly contradictory and very frightened business."
—COLIN HIGGINS, director (*Nine to Five*)

"Part of *Yentl*'s message was feminist, about equal access to education. It was disappointing that some female critics chose to be less than supportive, for instance writing and scoffing about 'designer yarmulkes.' It didn't deter me; it just made me aware that you cannot count on automatic support, no matter how logical that you should." —BARBRA STREISAND

"My father wouldn't go to see me in a [live] show. That was a blow to me, but it did make me stronger. You learn to rely on yourself more than on anyone else, and I suppose that's how it should be, but even so...." —BETTE MIDLER

"My father went to see me in one movie. He left before it was through. You could live to be 100 and that still hurts, but ... you push on. I'm sorry sometimes that I wasn't more the confrontational type, for my career's sake." —KIM NOVAK

"A shrink told me that avoiding problematic relatives was not good, because avoidance is not a choice.

"'What is it, then?' I asked.

"He said, 'It is leaving a problem unsolved.'

"How do you solve relatives who're down on you for being in show business and making 'dumb' career choices? The bottom line is my work makes me feel good; those relatives do not. To listen to a shrink, you'd have to be crazy!" —JOEY BISHOP (*Ocean's Eleven*)

"Being gay and ambitious, Tony Perkins decided early on not to do drag. So he turned down the hit movie *Some Like It Hot*. But he broke his own rule to do partial drag in a flop called *The Matchmaker*, which was *Hello, Dolly!* before they set it to music. . . . He also told me a leading man should 'always get the girl.' Broke his rule on that when he did *Psycho*, where he kills the girl. Of course that one was a big hit, but it pigeonholed him for keeps. Ever after, he's Norman Bates." —TIMMY EVERETT, actor and ex-lover of Perkins

"It is all too easy to fall into the comfortable and well-paid trap of repeating yourself. You can create your own stereotype, yes! After *The Mary Tyler Moore Show* and *Rhoda*, some individuals advised me I was through as an actor. I was Rhoda Morgenstern forever! Others opined that I should find new projects where I was again Rhoda or 'Rhoda-like.'

"Instead, I took roles in three media that were mostly opposites of Rhoda. I played glamorous, I played promiscuous, I played Golda Meir, I played Tallulah Bankhead, and yes, I even returned to Rhoda. My point—and I do have one, as darling Ellen DeGeneres says—is that if you're willing to make the effort, you will not be stereotyped and limited." —VALERIE HARPER

"There are a lot of lazy actors. They don't prepare hard enough . . . don't do their homework. Hey, homework doesn't stop with high school. And when the outcome is poor, they say, 'Well, I tried.' Don't say you tried. Do the real deal. They don't pay you for trying. They pay you for doing it right, for nailing it. If you don't, the next actor or the one after that will." —BRUCE PALTROW, TV producer-director (*St. Elsewhere*) and father of Gwyneth

"Don't use your habits as excuses or crutches. In some professions, you can. Maybe most. Not acting! If you're working regularly, this doesn't apply. But if you're not, then it's time to examine the habits and habitual attitudes that keep you from working more. Don't just explore character, as in fictional characters. Explore your own character, what your positives are and what your negatives are.

"Self-examination can be difficult, but for the actor it's usually necessary and it pays off." —PAUL WINFIELD (*Sounder*)

"It's been said before, but it's worth repeating: any habit that's been made can be unmade. Habits are not for life. Any habit can be broken. Break the ones that restrict you, your happiness, and your success." —HUME CRONYN (*The Gin Game*)

"Habit is a choice, one that you often don't know you've made. It can be a choice of physical appearance and behavior, or it can be a choice of attitude. . . . In a sense, habit determines who you are and how you live." —MILTON KATSELAS, acting coach

"The 'character' you have was not given you at birth. You developed it. You can choose to develop in any number of directions. As life is fairly short and you have only one, you, choose to develop in good and rewarding ways." —Sir BEN KINGSLEY (*Gandhi*)

"'Know thyself.' For nearly 2,500 years, since ancient Greece, this is some of the best advice for an actor. . . . Let's be practical. It's not about becoming a simple and simply wonderful person. It's about discovering and admitting your strengths and weaknesses, and then trying—and retrying—to make the changes that will best benefit you professionally." —PATRICIA NEAL, Oscar winner

"You're grown-up, right? Perhaps you had a lousy childhood and/or lousy parents. Well, it's over. If your parents weren't nice to you, that's past. Now you can be nice to you. Or are you going to keep from being nice to you because your parents, back then when you weren't in control of your own life, weren't nice to you? Hmm? Grow up!" —WILLIAM BELASCO, agent turned producer (*The Last Hard Man*)

"One's childhood is not a life sentence." —JOHN HARGREAVES, Australian actor

"I hear these young actors in class trying to explain, 'But they don't understand me,' or, 'I'm misunderstood.' Listen: nobody understands anybody else. *Capeesh?* Let's move on." —PEGGY FEURY, acting coach

"Some actors say that instead of going to a psychiatrist, we become other people. By playing different characters and comparing ourselves to them, and what we admire, what we deprecate, what we fear, we wind up understanding ourselves better. And don't have to pay for therapy!" —NATASHA RICHARDSON, actress daughter of Vanessa Redgrave and director Tony Richardson, and wife of Liam Neeson

"I come from a tight-knit, conservative Catholic family. What kind of girl would go for that? They were looking for the exotic, hot-blooded Cuban boys with skintight pants and forbidden dark-eyed lust. I presented myself as the wrong kind of guy. I was acting even at that age." —ANDY GARCIA

"I most enjoy the loss of self that can be achieved only through detailed understanding of another life." —DANIEL DAY-LEWIS, three-time Oscar winner

"I said I'd gotten tired of speaking someone else's words. But during [her retirement from acting while married to TV mogul Ted Turner] I did miss the mental stretches and psychological insights that come from acting. I missed the challenge and joy of creating and inhabiting a character, of living another life!" —JANE FONDA

"I was going through this dark night of the soul when I was 37. I thought, 'What did I ever do that thrilled me, that made me happy?' And it was acting. I thought, 'I've got to do it again.'" —JOHN MAHONEY (*Frasier*)

"You read that the biggest challenge for actors is finding work. True. Another big challenge is getting along with the diversity of personalities, ranks, and egos once you are working. And all their agendas." —EARTHA KITT

"Several directors have declared that 80 percent of success in acting is the ability to get along with people. Work on that! Acting is all about people—the people you act with, the people who watch you rehearse and act, and the people who pay to see you act." —NINA FOCH, actor-coach

"Relations can get tenser on a set when things are running behind. What other business is so expensive per minute, and where else do some individuals get paid millions for several weeks' work? It's not a business you can relax in for long, if at all. But just because manners aren't perfect and moodiness emerges and tempers may flare and erupt, keep your cool—it's usually not meant personally. It's just the nature of the beast." —CHICO DAY, the first Mexican-American assistant director to join the Directors Guild of America, and brother of actor Gilbert Roland

"So many actors get hung up on perfection. First, it doesn't exist. Not in any definable, universally accepted way. It's a concept—an opinion. Mostly, it's a barrier. Parents, teachers, directors, and others have urged you toward perfection, supposedly wanting you to do your best. But in fact, it's more about conforming to their standards, pleasing them, and not embarrassing them." —JOSEPH WISEMAN (*Dr. No*)

"To blazes with perfection, whatever that be. Do your best, and infuse it with passion." —ELSIE FOGERTY, who founded London's Central School of Speech and Drama in 1906

"My hands were badly burnt in a fire. After several operations, they still didn't look good, and were clumsy. Not a typical actress's hands . . . I lost the middle joint on my right hand's little finger, so I couldn't bend it any more. But I wasn't about to give up acting . . . I developed a hand makeup for the stage, lending them contour, shading, highlights. I tested them to see which positions looked best. Then I used them, constantly and with diminishing self-consciousness. Until one day I stopped noticing them.

"Do you know, it wasn't until long after my hands were burned that I received requests from sculptors, painters, and photographers to mold, portray, and capture my hands? Before the accident, no one ever thought my hands were special." —EVA LE GALLIENNE, stage producer and actress who was Oscar-nominated for *Resurrection*

"Adversity builds character." —LEO TOLSTOY, novelist (*Anna Karenina, War and Peace*)

"I go to the gym regularly, but I don't know if steroids help build muscle. But I know energy drinks aren't the way to go for building and maintaining stamina or coping with a difficult assignment. Don't get to relying too much on anything outside yourself. As an actor, you should be developing your inner resources first and foremost. They're definitely enough to carry you through." —RUPERT EVERETT (*My Best Friend's Wedding*)

"Actors search for answers and help. To some degree, we all need this. But for the most part, don't overemphasize or become addicted to any one thing, person, or way." —WHOOPI GOLDBERG

"Are you living a script written by somebody else? You have to write your own script. You have to discover your own values, your own viewpoints, your own passions." —MILTON KATSELAS, acting coach

"Nothing anyone does can ever please everyone. So tailor your effort to the situation at hand, give it your all, and don't be afraid to soar. Don't let your assumptions about *their* reactions inhibit or embarrass you." —MEL BLANC, the voice of Bugs Bunny, Porky the Pig, Daffy Duck, etc.

"I used to hear it a lot: 'He doesn't smile enough.' It bothered me. Not smiling didn't mean I was unhappy, it was just . . . my expression. I felt what came out of my mouth mattered more than what was on it. Anyway, I did not become a smiler, and I've enjoyed a pretty decent career." —PAUL BURKE (*Valley of the Dolls*)

"Early on, I was expected to be perky. Like, all the time! As I got older, too. . . . Remembering to be perky and wear that smile, and to giggle now and then, can distract you from your lines and inner expression. . . . With time and confidence, I grew into my own mode of performance and being. Of which perky is just one facet." —GOLDIE HAWN

"It is so much worse for actresses, with the constant zooming in on your looks. And how you present them. I'd think, *Should I cross my legs? Tilt my head a bit when I'm listening? Turn the left knee inward while stand-ing?* So many things, so many thoughts! Sometimes I'd freeze—easier to be a model or a statue. But I sup-pose it's a phase actors have to go through, and then gradually or suddenly one is freed." —ELIZABETH HURLEY, model turned actor

"Don't ponder too much. Thinking can get in an actor's way. By the way, this applies to non-actors too. If there's a thing to be done or a problem to overcome, okay, weigh the pros and cons. But not [for] too long! After that, just . . . do it!" —CLORIS LEACHMAN, Oscar winner

"I used to hesitate to talk to a director, even when I thought I knew better. But don't we all know better? I figured the director's got everything figured out. You're just an actor. There's no such thing as 'just' an actor, but it wasn't till I became a director that I learned how helpful an unexpected good suggestion can be. Sometimes it can make a big difference." —BURT REYNOLDS

"If you have a great suggestion, try putting it across as a way to help the whole project, not specifically as your idea. I've found that directors often welcome smart suggestions, particularly if they're tactfully made so that the director can share in the credit. Hell, even if he doesn't share it, he'll know, and he may come back to you for more ideas . . . may hire you again." —RICHARD KILEY (*Ally McBeal*)

"It's easier on you if you share concerns or suggestions in a way that shows your aim is to solve problems, not create them. Show that you don't want to argue, but to contribute positively to solving a problem, and that you're not out to prove somebody wrong and make yourself look good. Be sincere. But if you hate the director's guts, then *act* sincere." —HERMAN COHEN, producer (*I Was a Teenage Werewolf*)

"Actors take classes in communicating on stage and on camera with their scene partners. They need classes in better communication with crews, including, naturally, directors. Most actors either stall, not saying anything out of fear, or they create a confrontation that by its nature is self-defeating. But then, a lot of actors have trouble with authority figures." —TIM FLACK, CBS Vice President of Creative Affairs

"I was doing a movie based on a very popular book. The novelist came to visit one day. For the few hours he was there, he all but took over from the director, flinging opinions and suggestions about like confetti. When he left, I asked the director, 'What makes him such an authority?' The director asked, 'What are the first six letters in "authority"?'"—Sir JOHN MILLS

"Two kinds of books for actors. . . . Those by the great acting gurus add dimension and inspiration to your knowledge of acting—they're in most libraries. Practical ones with the scoop and suggestions about photos, résumés, auditioning, Internet submissions, etc.—they're pretty crucial. Libraries don't always have the latest ones—that's when you head for the bookstore." —KATHY BATES (*Misery*)

"I've had the pleasure of reading more than once that I'm a great actor. Then one day, in my unexpected middle age, I read, 'still a great actor.' That five-letter 'still'. . . . Still, I reminded myself, some have never been described as great. So that's all right then." —MAURICE EVANS, Shakespearean actor best known as Samantha's father on *Bewitched*

"My father was conflicted and confused about wanting me to be a star. Jealousy can run deep in families, and I was a fairly successful child actor. . . . My main objection to kids acting is that they see too much too soon. Their un-perplexed innocence vanishes. This is anything but an innocent, gentle business." —ROBERT BLAKE

"Adulthood makes us jaded anyway . . . the life of an actor makes anybody more jaded. But a tip: don't let yourself get too jaded—it'll show in your work. I promise you. Not in every scene, but it'll at least peek through and will detract from the quality of your work and the appeal of your persona." —EILEEN HECKART, Oscar winner (*Butterflies Are Free*)

"Keep a sense of wonder. Stay curious. Don't settle into a permanent niche. Wonder about why the Mayas abandoned their magnificent cities. Ask about the new sound equipment you see being used. Don't take it for granted. If someone mentions their kid had a birthday, ask what kind of cake and how many guests. Keep your world and your senses open." —RUSSELL JOHNSON, Professor on *Gilligan's Island*

"One thing I do is, when I have a negative thought, right away I come up with a positive one. Whatever it may be—a pet, some flowers I recently saw, a fond childhood memory, a handsome guy that smiled at me or that I smiled at. . . ." —TERI HATCHER (*Desperate Housewives*)

"It's probably like a law of physics—for every negative, there's a positive. My kids moved out, okay, so: empty nest, full fridge." —JACKIE STALLONE, mother of actors Frank and Sylvester

"Don't look for a lover. Be one. Then they'll come to you. Same principle applies to acting." —JAMES LEO HERLIHY, novelist (*Midnight Cowboy*)

"A little cheerfulness wouldn't hurt." —BORIS ARONSON, theater designer

"My goodness, the solemnity with which some New York actors approach their work! There's a blond American actor, first name William—you'd think he was preparing for heart-transplant surgery, he's so serious. I felt like telling him, the

day I visited the set, 'It's only acting, chum.'"
—ROBERT VAN SCOYK, TV writer-producer
(*Murder, She Wrote*)

"The fear of losing something, such as dignity, makes you less effective towards it. The actor or executive terrified of losing his dignity often comes off as pompous, even humorous. He is less naturally dignified than one who knows, who has confidence, that he's dignified. If he loses his dignity for a few seconds or minutes, he knows it's temporary. It's only the situation; he doesn't become an undignified individual. The secret is to lessen your fear of losing whatever it is." —JOAN LITTLEWOOD, London stage producer (*A Taste of Honey*)

"My fear isn't death. My fear is not using my life, the time that I have, to fullest or at least good advantage. Time is the most valuable commodity we have, and the one we squander the most." —LOIS MAXWELL, Miss Moneypenny in 14 James Bond movies

"You're always hearing someone say they just don't have time for such-and-such; they wish they did. Who are they fooling? We each make time for what we want to do or enjoy doing. Haven't got time to exercise 30 minutes every other day? Then how come you spend two or three hours per day watching television? Everyone makes time for what they want to make time for." —JUDY LEWIS, former actress, and daughter via costar Clark Gable of Loretta Young, who for 31 years claimed Judy was "adopted"

"In the time of your life, live." —WILLIAM SAROYAN, writer (*The Time of Your Life*)

"A performer can escape reality in her work. That's what draws many people to acting. But in your life, and increasingly as you get older, deal with reality. Deal with it so you can improve things—for yourself and your career and for others.

"Time doesn't stand still, but if you do, you'll get left behind and become anachronistic. I know older actresses who still wear the long hairdos they did in their twenties. It looks grizzly, but no one tells them to their face what they really look like or the sad or jarring impression they make." —PENNY SINGLETON, star of 28 *Blondie* movies and president of the Screen Actors Guild

"Don't be afraid to flatter others, but take stock before you flatter yourself. Reality must be dealt with sooner or later." —ALIDA VALLI (*The Third Man*)

"*An optimist or a pessimist?* One gets asked. I feel either answer is unrealistic, since life bountifully justifies both outlooks, but neither alone. When the question arises, I don't hesitate: 'A realist.'" —PETER FINCH, who posthumously won an Academy Award for *Network*

"Ultimately one absorbs the lesson that life, including people, is not an either/or proposition. It is and/but."
—KAM FONG (*Hawaii Five-O*)

"My biggest complaint about actors, that I don't dwell on while working, is how so many think that 'compromise' means giving in. To what? Cooperation? If you're a painter and I tell you to do it a different way, fine, don't compromise.

"But filmmaking is a cooperation of people, plural, and if I tell you to act it differently or to adjust something, are you the director? Do you have the overall picture in mind or just your part?" —JOHN FRANKENHEIMER, director

"I find the bigger, established stars are more mature. When I have problem actors, typically they're younger males. Insecure, angry-and-afraid, would-be macho. . . . They lecture and complain about their 'scruples' and how they refuse to compromise them. Dandy. We'll just get someone else who doesn't confuse arrogance with 'scruples.'"
—J. LEE THOMPSON, director (*Cape Fear*)

"Some actors actually enjoy their moaning and whining. If you do, which some people won't admit even to themselves, then stay with your bitchy bunch. But if you prefer positive action to negative listening and grumbling, then dump the flotsam and sail onward." —ANN DOLLARD, Leading Artists agent

"To cope well, you have to consider the glass as half full. What's the use of the other point of view? You do get to choose, and it can affect everything." —Dame JUDI DENCH

"I asked Sir Johnny [John Gielgud] when he was about 90 if he thought the glass was half full of water or half empty? He said, 'I'm more interested in the shape and make of the glass, dear boy.'" —DUDLEY MOORE

"Never completely forget that some people have hardly any water at all." —Dr. HAING S. NGOR (*The Killing Fields*)